THE UNPERFECT SOCIETY

BEYOND THE NEW CLASS

MILOVAN DJILAS

THE
UNPERFECT
SOCIETY

BEYOND
THE
NEW CLASS

Translated by Dorian Cooke

Harcourt, Brace & World, Inc., New York

A BIOGRAPHICAL NOTE ON
MILOVAN DJILAS

Milovan Djilas was born in 1911 in Montenegro, the stark fateful land he describes in the autobiography of his youth, *Land Without Justice*. He lives today in Belgrade, having spent about a third of his adult life in prison. He came to Belgrade as a university student in 1929 and soon became a Communist organizer, a role that led to his being tortured and to his imprisonment for three years by the Royalist government. By the time he was twenty-seven he was a member of the Central Committee of the Communist party in Yugoslavia, and in 1940 he became a member of its Politburo. When Germany invaded his country, he became a Partisan fighter and leader, and as a Partisan general he led a military mission to Moscow in 1944. The following year, as a minister in Tito's postwar Communist government, he went again to Moscow for talks with Stalin and other Soviet leaders. In 1948 he once again headed a mission to Moscow, this time in a vain attempt to avoid the break between the two Communist states that was to occur later in the same year. Once the break was made, Djilas became the expositor of Yugoslavia's position as an "independent"

Communist state and stated the case for "national Communism" in postwar Eastern Europe.

Ideological disagreements between the party leadership in Yugoslavia and Milovan Djilas began in 1953. He had written articles critical of the governmental bureaucracy that he was soon to call the "new class," and in January of 1954 he was expelled from the Central Committee of the party. During this period of conflict and "exile" he devoted himself to writing *The New Class,* a brilliant analysis of Communist oligarchy, and *Land Without Justice,* the manuscripts for both books having been sent to publishers before his arrest by the Tito regime. The year following his official break with the party, 1955, found Djilas being tried and sentenced (a sentence of three years was passed but suspended) for creating "hostile propaganda"; this charge arose from an interview he gave to the New York *Times.* After the uprising in Hungary, he publicly criticized the Yugoslav government's failure to denounce the Soviet Union's invasion of that country, and he was now imprisoned at Sremska Mitrovica, the same Serbian prison where he had earlier served time as an eager young Communist and where, until 1967, he was to spend a total of nine years as a critic of Communism. The publication of *The New Class* in 1957 caused Djilas to be brought from prison to undergo a new trial, which resulted in an increase of his sentence. *Land Without Justice* was published in 1958.

From 1956 until he was conditionally released in January of 1961, Djilas spent his time in prison writing, despite his being subjected to twenty months of solitary confinement. He produced a massive authoritative biography of Njegoš, the great Montenegrin prince-poet-priest (*Njegoš,* published in 1966); a fictional and historical account of Montenegro during the First World War (*Montenegro,* published in

1963); sixteen tales (*The Leper and Other Stories,* published in 1964). Upon his release in 1961, Djilas wrote a work describing his meetings with Stalin, and during that year mailed the manuscript to his American publisher. Once again the Yugoslav regime moved against him as a writer, and he was arrested in April of 1962; soon afterward he was brought to trial on charges of having published information he had obtained as an official of the government. (The law under which he was tried was passed on March 17, 1962, but the existence of his manuscript had been publicly known earlier.) *Conversations with Stalin* was published in May of 1962, following a fruitless attempt on the part of his American publisher to secure his release. Djilas was returned to the Sremska Mitrovica prison under an extended sentence, and remained there until the last day of 1966, when he was unconditionally released but placed under a restriction against his making public statements for five years.

During Djilas's second imprisonment under the Tito regime he resumed his writing under the most trying conditions. Although he was, this time, spared a period of solitary confinement, he was for almost two years denied writing paper—he actually wrote on toilet paper—and throughout this term lived and wrote in a cell that was daily unheated except for a brief evening period. Yet he managed to produce the manuscripts for four books: a novel titled *Lost Battles* (to be published in 1970); a volume of tales, *The Violets and the Stone* (also to be published in 1970); a translation of Milton's *Paradise Lost* into Serbo-Croatian, which is the first such translation (to be published in 1969); a novel titled *Worlds and Bridges,* which is being revised by the author and is not at present scheduled for publication. Following his release, Djilas set to work on *The Unperfect Society: Beyond The New Class,* which he delivered to his publisher on October 13, 1968, upon his arrival in New York for a stay of two months in the United States.

Djilas lives under a ban not to publish any writings until 1972. Following his release he applied several times to the officials to relieve him of this prohibition and to grant him a passport so that he might travel abroad. Although he was given a pension and although he was—quite suddenly during the Czechoslovak crisis—given a passport to travel to Great Britain and the United States, he has not been relieved of the prohibition to publish. Nonetheless, Milovan Djilas has proceeded to arrange with his publisher to issue during 1969 *The Unperfect Society: Beyond The New Class* and his Serbo-Croatian translation of *Paradise Lost,* neither of which will be available in Yugoslavia. He returned to Belgrade on December 10, 1968 to stay with his wife and son. During his stay in the United States (his first visit to this country since 1949, when he attended the United Nations as a Yugoslav representative), Djilas served as a Fellow in Public and International Affairs of the Woodrow Wilson School of Public and International Affairs at Princeton University, and lived at Princeton for the larger part of his stay. It is an irony of circumstance, if not of history, that at Princeton he could visit his neighbors, M. Svetlana Alliluyeva, the daughter of Stalin, and George Kennan, who was ambassador to Yugoslavia from the United States when Djilas was arrested because of *Conversations with Stalin.* The day before his departure for his native country, Djilas was given the Freedom Award of Freedom House, and as its recipient thereby joined Pablo Casals, Jean Monnet, and Sir Winston Churchill, among others.

The importance of Milovan Djilas's reflections on the philosophical and pragmatic aspects of Communism is heightened not only by the personal suffering he has undergone for making them known, but also by his direct experience as an administrator in a Communist state. At the time of his break with the Yugoslav Communist party, he was one of the four main leaders of the Yugoslav regime. These were: Tito himself, Djilas (who was widely considered to be Tito's eventual successor), Kardelj, and Ranković (who was in 1966 deposed by Tito, allegedly for deploying the secret police under his control "illegally"). Between 1945 and 1954 Djilas was at various times a minister, Vice President of the nation, President of its Federal Assembly. With Moša Pijade, another early party member in Yugoslavia, Dijlas became the government's best-known spokesman and propagandist for Communist doctrine. After his expulsion from the Central Committee and his resignation from the party, Djilas began alone the long period, lasting fifteen years, of devolving and expressing ideas for a freer, more multifarious life, in the unperfect but amenable, improvable society of men.

THE PUBLISHER

THE UNPERFECT SOCIETY

BEYOND THE NEW CLASS

INTRODUCTION

These introductory remarks would have been unnecessary if I had not had to overcome political obstacles before my ideas could finally appear in print.

I had just finished writing *The New Class* when, in November 1956, I was clapped into jail by the Yugoslav authorities for making statements and for publishing articles in defense of the Hungarian uprising. All my instincts and energies, my memories and dreams, were still throbbing with the life that I left outside the prison walls. I had to keep these on a leash and inure myself to loneliness, rejection, and slow death. In all this turmoil my thoughts kept their course until, filtered and clarified, they found their release within the steel and concrete walls of a cell in Belgrade's Central Prison.

With *The New Class* completed, I felt, as things were, a sudden upsurge of yearning for fresh creative work, and new visions and themes for it. These creative urges were the more compelling because I became aware that, while the book provided only a critical appraisal of the society which I had helped to bring into being and in which I had to live, it gave scant treatment to future prospects and possible alternatives. As a matter of fact, in the undergrowth of dogma and the darkness of unbelief which I had penetrated I had been nowhere near the kernel of a solution. In a curious way, I was unable to set to work on the book I was planning to write because I had not yet found a title for it. Before I could actually get my mind on the details, the theme of the book had to become crystallized inside me verbally—in the shape of a title.

Three or four days of my imprisonment passed. One day, on my way to the prison yard, a concrete quadrangle surrounded by five-storied blocks where I exercised for an hour in the afternoons, it suddenly occurred to me that the book I was contemplating ought to be called *The Unperfect Society:* it would be an antithesis to the perfect, or classless, society by which Communists justified the continuation of their dictatorship and their own privileged position. Under the dingy canopy of a November sky my footsteps rang out in the concrete void of the yard, hammering into my brain the words "Unperfect Society" . . . "Unperfect Society" . . .

I need perhaps to explain here my use of the word "unperfect," with which I seek to make a semantic distinction from the more common "imperfect." As the chapters that follow will illustrate, it is my belief that society cannot be perfect. Men must hold both ideas and ideals, but they should not regard these as being wholly realizable. We need to comprehend the nature of utopianism. Utopianism, once it achieves power, becomes dogmatic, and it quite readily can create human suffering in the name and in the cause of its own scientism and idealism. To speak of society as imperfect may seem to imply that it *can* be perfect, which in truth it cannot. The task for contemporary man is to accept the reality that society is unperfect, but also to understand that humanist, humanitarian dreams and visions are necessary in order to reform society, in order to improve and advance it.

In my prison diary and the notes I had kept during my first imprisonment (1956–1961) in postwar Yugoslavia can be found, without difficulty, in spite of the resentful and frustrated manner in which they were expressed, the propositions upon which this present book is based.[1] On coming out of prison in January 1961 I had gone ahead trying to get the book into shape—jotting down ideas, collecting data, drafting an outline. But fortune still frowned upon me and upon this scheme of mine, or perhaps I was not yet compelled strongly enough to express myself. However that may be, I was soon arrested by the Yugoslav regime again, because of the impending publication of my book *Conversations with Stalin*. Another five years of imprisonment passed, but my determination to write the book, though pushed into the background and neglected, was never abandoned. The tales and novels, no less than the notes and diaries, I wrote in prison during this period (1962–1966) certainly contain more than a glimmer of the ideas in *The Unperfect Society*. The quietude of my prison life, and my own

1. These documents were not returned to me by the authorities, in 1961, but, rather, in 1967, after I was released from my second postwar imprisonment.

tranquillity, allowed the ideas to ripen with self-assurance and without bitterness. I nurtured them, and I still nurture them, as the deepest revelation of all that I am and all that I aspire to achieve. Now that I have disposed of matters that are important to my family and myself, I have gone forward with the writing and publication of the book.

And so, if *The New Class* is the description of a collectively heroic and tragic experience, *The Unperfect Society* is the mature fruit of solitary and patient contemplation.

But, without waiting for theories, time has done its work, and new patterns have appeared in society, so that *The Unperfect Society,* conceived in 1956 as a sequel to *The New Class,* is now a more cohesive and self-contained work than it would have been if written earlier. Perhaps it is as well that things have turned out in this way. At the time, in the middle of the nineteen-fifties, the changes in the society that had been depicted in *The New Class* were still tentative, undefined: their future course could not be predicted with any reliability. It is not my intention to make predictions now. Still other changes have occurred in the meanwhile, and these changes will, in turn, give impetus to new ideas and to new undertakings.

It is not these changes in the world, however, that I wish to write about. My departure from my original conception of *The Unperfect Society,* as a sequel to *The New Class,* obliges me to turn back to *The New Class* in order to see how far it is different from, if not actually inconsistent with, my new book. Moreover, time has flaked the gilt, and made nonsense of the anathemas, which a specific moment in history placed upon the book; and the facts of life itself have effaced the blueprints and marked paid to the "ultimate truths" which had given it its character as an ideological work.

In this introduction I shall not be referring in any detail to *The New Class;* the changes in my thinking, or, rather, in the state of affairs I am depicting, will be apparent to the informed and discriminating reader of *The Unperfect Society* in the actual text. I think, though, that I should draw attention to two points.

First, in *The New Class* I still had recourse to the Marxist standpoint and methodology. In essence, *The New Class* is a Marxist critique of contemporary Communism. I did, however, realize, at the time, that I was beginning to erode the Marxist method, because in fact I was laying bare the reality of Communist, Marxist, society. Occasionally, while writing *The New Class,* I would be seized by a strange and demonic delight in the havoc I was wreaking on my own work and beliefs. (I remember writing sentences and whole pages in a subconscious frenzy, with visions of teeming masses mobilizing themselves and throwing themselves into battle, carried away by my words and the truths revealed in them.) In *The New Class,* the Marxist dialectic, by insisting on its achievements, becomes corroded at the core and negates its own potential. Like the heretic, I was only capable of revealing the incongruities of Communist realities with the help of visions, prognostications, and pledges culled from Marxist holy writ. Thus, the Hegelian-Marxist dialectical method, still a sharp and attractive tool for scraping bare the contradictions in the society for which it is made to serve as a spiritual weapon, has shown itself to-day to be inadequate in the search for alternatives and new social patterns. If, in spite of this, traces of the Marxist method and Marxist outlook are still to be found in this book, the explanation lies in my respect for those Marxist achievements that, albeit in a modified form, have become part of modern social science and modern thinking—for example, the possibility of change in social patterns, the inevitability of internal contradictions in every society, the importance of economic factors in society and human life, the treatment of society as an object of scientific research. If traces persist, then some part of Marxism also lies in my conscious and unconscious efforts to remain in touch with vital issues in my own country and the society to which I am pledged.

Second, the Marxist method may not have played a big part in helping me to reach my basic proposition in *The New Class*, but it was important in the actual elaboration of that proposition, so today an explanation is called for. As everyone who has read *The New Class* knows, the proposition proceeds as follows: the society that has arisen as the result of Communist revolutions, or as a result of the military actions of the Soviet Union, is torn by the same sort of contradictions as are other societies. The result is that the Communist society has not only failed to develop toward human brotherhood and equality, but also out of its party bureaucracy there arises a privileged social stratum, which, in accord with Marxist thinking, I named "the new class." I am unable to make myself completely familiar with all the well-intentioned and learned criticisms made against this thesis, although

I know they exist in the United States and in Western Europe. In the socialist countries, the thesis, like the book itself, has been either passed over in silence or else distorted. I would say that objections to my thesis can be reduced to the following: the continuance and mobility of a society—particularly the society in a socialist country, where it is not compartmentalized on the basis of formal ownership, as were former societies—cannot be subordinated to any formula, even a Marxist one; nor can the changes in society be explained exclusively on the basis of its class structure.

In an indirect criticism of me, Professor Ralf Dahrendorf [2] has, in my view, shown that the very definition of class as something final and immutable in society, particularly a modern society, is untenable and unsound, and inevitably leads to purely academic approaches to society. In other words, only an analysis that does not proceed from *a priori* "truths" or "ultimately revealed laws" can, to some extent, offer a real picture of a given society and allow one to hazard conjectures about trends likely to occur in it. Without disputing such an approach to society, and therefore to *The New Class*, I wish to stress one thing: insofar as there are, as there must be, rather schematic approaches in *The New Class*, they must be ascribed not only to the Marxist method which still beset me at that time, but also to my desire to expose the Communist social system *by means of the theory on which it relies spiritually*.

Although at the time I was already aware that Marx

2. *Class and Class Conflict in Industrial Society*, Stanford, California, 1959.

9

and Lenin cannot provide explanations for many contemporary phenomena that would satisfy even Communists, their teachings still forced themselves upon me as the most suitable tool for uncovering the incongruities between Communist theory and practice. Thus *The New Class,* by showing that a society inspired by Marxist doctrine not only fails to conform to it, but also actually develops away from it in a different direction, foreshadows the inadequacy of Marxist teaching for the modern world, particularly, and this is specially significant, for the East European and other Communist countries. Therefore, the phrase "the new class" should be taken as no more than a conditional and conditioned term for the new privileged ruling strata in the so-called socialist countries whose existence and ethos, as described in *The New Class,* no serious and impartial critic has denied. If the truth be told, I was not, in fact, the first to use the term. At the time of writing *The New Class* I was unaware that N. J. Bukharin, Bertrand Russell, and N. A. Berdyev had used it much earlier to describe the same general social phenomenon, though they were much more predictive about it than analytical. Further, in Yugoslavia, Kristl and Stanovnik had pointed out not long before the publication of *The New Class* (in an argument with me, as a matter of fact) that the bureaucracy under socialism constituted a class. However, they do not today express such views, now that these comprise so wicked a heresy.

This, then, is how I would look back at the method and views expressed in *The New Class,* and how I would regard the unpartisan, scientific examination of both and, finally, of the book itself.

But in order to give the reader a more complete picture of my political views, and my attitude to other kinds of criticism, I shall pay some attention to criticism from certain circles and groups for whom anti-Communism is the wellspring and fount of all spiritual life, and also to the lack of criticism in the ranks of the Communists.

The first kind of criticism reached me from the ranks of anti-Communist Yugoslavs and Russian émigrés. Their thesis is roughly this: everything that Djilas has published in *The New Class* and elsewhere has long been well known to us; nevertheless it is useful to hear it from one who was until quite recently a Communist leader and ideologist. Now I have no intention of checking the reliability of anyone's knowledge of a given society, even if such a thing could be done. But the presumed knowledge of these émigré warriors and ideologists seems suspect to me, not merely because it is distorted by an *a priori* schematic approach, but even more because it devolves from their own historical defeats. Although I consider myself a principal critic of the social role and ideas of the Communist bureaucracy, I have never considered myself to be an anti-Communist; nor have I been one, at least not in the sense that these critics and all anti-Communist crusaders are. *The New Class* is fired with the vehemence of an embattled man and the bitterness of an ex-Communist potentate; yet not even here, or in any other of my works, have Communist systems been treated as merely the product of a fortuitous concatenation of circumstances or of diabolic powers. No, in *The New Class*, as in my other works, I point out the conditions that gave birth to those forces able and willing to fight for Communist systems and to keep them in power. I have avoided making predictions—particularly any specific intimations about modifications in, or the replacement of, Communist systems. My point of view is that they are inescapable phenomena, in that they have actually appeared and do exist, so that any substantial modification in such a system can only arise out of the system itself. And even if there really were categories of absolute good and absolute evil, rather than the doomsday pledges of men committed to fight for visionary ideals, it would be nonsensical and pointless to evaluate Communist systems exclusively by these standards, and even more so to use them for strategy and tactics against Communist bureaucracy or (worse yet) against Communism as a whole. Good or bad (and I believe the longer the systems last, the worse they become, because in their present state they are becoming an increasing burden to their own peoples), these systems by their very endurance influenced the whole human race; they are as much a reality as any other system, so that attitudes to them should be free from fantasy and wishful thinking, from hatred or from sentimental nostalgia. In other words, those who fail to understand the determinacy and inevitability of Communism's triumph in certain countries must in fact lack faith in the possibility of its changing, and so they cannot be capable of finding forces and means within the system to fight it.

As for the willful disregard of *The New Class* and my

other works, even fiction, and the ban on them in the Communist countries, more telling than any argument is the fact that *The New Class* has been illegally copied and circulated from hand to hand throughout Eastern Europe, that in the Soviet Union free-thinking people are thrown into jail because of it. Moreover, in Yugoslavia today hardly anyone can be found, even in the ruling circles, who is so unreasonable as to maintain that antagonisms and various social groups, including privileged ones, do not exist in socialist systems, so that there is reason to hope that some courageous people will draw practical conclusions from what they learn. In this connection, I must stress that officials in the Communist countries, and first and foremost in my fatherland, are faced with a peculiar dilemma. Being unable to explain my "treachery," they have been forced to ignore my views elaborately and to keep quiet about their own behavior toward me.

It is not my intention to take up the question of witch hunts and excommunications, whose purpose is merely to intimidate anyone who might be tempted to follow in the footsteps of "apostates" like myself. There are Communist and non-Communist simpletons who have been taken in by the slander that I turned against Communism from tarnished motives, and kept silent about the faults of the Western countries and their systems. I feel I owe them an explanation—all the more so since the charge contains a grain of truth while remaining the most abominable falsehood. In the days when, like all good dogmatists, I maintained that a knowledge of Marxist doctrine provided insight into and knowledge of all human societies in the world, not merely one's own, I used to criticize capitalism, *i.e.*, Western systems and Western states. After a while I realized that my knowledge of them was insufficient; and so I maintain that it is more appropriate for the people who live in those countries to comment on conditions there and, ultimately, to change them. But this does not mean that I have no opinions, even superficial ones, about these societies. Nor does it mean, obviously, that these societies, or some Western country in particular, are the source of my ideas for remedies and social patterns in my own country or any other Communist state. Nowadays I am eager to learn from any quarter, and I endeavor to admit any mistakes I may have made involving other people. Nevertheless, I do not forget that the Balkan nations have survived for centuries, stretched out between East and West, by establishing their distinctive character precisely as a synthesis between their own and outside, between native and alien, social patterns and aspirations. It seems to me that nothing could be more cosmopolitan and portentous for these nations than to make a bridge with other nations regardless of their systems and ideologies, while keeping their own identity. Nothing can be loftier and nobler for their striving and creative sons than to remain open to all the winds—to find their own answers.

I must also mention that there have been still other objections from diverse quarters: namely, that my thinking, like my personality, is controversial and inconsistent. It is certainly no easy task to follow or understand the reckless adventures that led the Communist revolutionary, the Marxist theoretician and Stalinist practitioner, to rebel against Stalin, then against his own system, and finally, now, against the ideology itself. But such objections can be leveled not only against much greater rebels and heretics of history, but also, literally, against all pioneers. Would it not, therefore, be more plausible to seek the explanation for these contradictions in the storms of our times and in the conditions under which I had to live my life and express myself? It is certainly easier for me to accept any kind of reproach than it is to fail to be true to myself. My own objection to this kind of reproach—that I am at times contradictory—is that it ignores the fact that I have never tackled the problem of building an ideological system in my writings but have, rather, sought to expand human perspectives and the understanding of human destiny by shedding light on moments in my times and on patterns in my environment.

And today, as I write these words, I can feel the driving force of the same innate or acquired longing for the good that cast me in my youth into the crater of revolution, and that in my mature years put my mind and conscience, the whole of my personality, to the test. Today, as in the days of my youth and of the recent past, I have more reason to believe I shall be slandered and persecuted because of this book than that I shall not—though I have had the chance, for the past two years, to live in relative comfort and in the tranquillity and warmth of my family.

The need for self-expression, the expression of one's thoughts, enthusiasms, and visions, is as compelling as the will to live itself. . . . For striving and creating, for the impulse to creative striving, there is no end.

Finally, I have to say something about the direct and more profound motives behind this book, which have imposed themselves upon me from a desire to be a witness of my times.

All the demons that Communism believed it had banished from the forthcoming as well as the real world have crept into the soul of Communism and become part of its being. Communism, once a popular movement that in the name of science inspired the toiling and oppressed people of the world with the hope of creating the Kingdom of Heaven on earth, that launched, and continues to launch, millions to their deaths in pursuit of this unextinguishable primeval dream, has become transformed into national political bureaucracies and states squabbling among themselves for prestige and influence, for the sources of wealth and for markets—for all those things over which politicians and governments have always quarreled, and always will. The Communists were compelled by their own ideas and by the realities in their society first to wrest power—that delight above all delights—from their opponents, and then scrabble for it among themselves. This has been the fate of all revolutionary movements in history. The Communists became so completely absorbed and engulfed in greed and the lust for power that their power became absolute, totalitarian; and in their struggle for power they showed themselves to be ordinary mortals, as fallible as other men, rather than initiates of "a special mold," as Stalin called them. Moreover, Communism, in building up regimes over peoples with diverse destinies and opportunities, was forced to abandon its own international centers, which is to say

Moscow and Peking, because in our times these were bound to become great powers in their own right. By donning its national garb and traveling its national roads, Communism was brought into uncharted paths and, indeed, calamities. It was actually from seeds sown on national soil that strife and dissension proliferated in every shape and over every area—as must have been inevitable in a movement that presumed to offer a total explanation of the world and to impose a totalitarian sway over human existence. The economies that the Communists had supposed would "consciously" and "according to plan" bring about the "abolition of production for the market" and lead to "consumption according to need"—and, thereafter, according to Lenin, to gold's being debased in an alloy to be used for lavatory pans— seek their salvation today in the free market and in the international valuation of gold. Instead of abolishing war, as the Communists once believed was possible, portending it with their victories, now the great Communist powers have enslaved smaller Communist countries, and the human race is under the threat of a conflict between the two great Communist powers, the Soviet Union and China, a conflict no less probable, and no less perilous, than a conflict between them and the powers of the "old order"—the "saviors" of humanity engaging in internecine war, the "happiness-makers" being compelled to look after their own skins. . . .

The human race will lose nothing as a result of this Communist cataclysm, although it will be presented to the scattered ranks of the Communist faithful as the Last Trump of Judgment Day. Even the Communists will survive; because although the society prophesied by the Communist teachers has not come into being, Communists as individuals—and to some extent Communism as a movement—are undergoing a change and adapting themselves to what society can and must be.

The Communists are chiefly to blame for their own misfortunes. The result of their obstinacy in pursuing an imaginary society, in the belief that they could change human nature, is that their ideas and they themselves have been inexorably crunched by the frenzy of the violence they perpetrated. The human being under Communism, as in all situations at all times in human history, has proved too intractable and quite unfit for any ideal models, particularly those that seek to restrict his boundaries and prescribe his destiny.

In spite of all this, however, the enemies of Communism will deceive themselves if they rejoice prematurely. Certainly any attempt on their part to exploit the work and suffering and struggles of enslaved peoples—and the few free spirits who dare to speak out among them— would be unfeasible and shortsighted. For, on the other side, too, the non-Communist side, many changes are taking place. If only the people of our time could break away from the ideological frameworks they have inherited, from the illusions and the still-active divisions and antagonisms, they would be able to say with a clear conscience that capitalism and Communism are no more, at least they no longer exist either in Western or in Eastern Europe. If West European capitalism, which was described by Marx and whose downfall he predicted, has not in fact disappeared, it has changed so greatly that it no more resembles its adolescent image than, on the other side of the coin, contemporary East European Communism resembles the blessed classless society of Marx's dreams. Capitalist and socialist model societies no longer exist. As a matter of fact, they never did exist except in the visions repeated faithfully by academics or dreamers and in the gall-constricted and distorted accounts of revolutionary fighters, which have, for the most part, ended in the sterile but nonetheless terrifying experiments of despots holding sway over human beings and human communities. The concepts Communism, capitalism, even socialism—insofar as it does not mean freer personalities, greater rights for social groups, and a more equitable distribution of goods than obtains at present—all belong to earlier ages. And the reason people in the East and in the West still come across these concepts, and why, by all accounts, they will have to contend with them for a long time to come, is to be found in the fact that ideas are like vampires; ideas are capable of living after the death of the generations and social conditions in and by which they were inspired. Today such vampire ideas persist in the spiritual delirium and putrefaction of contemporary social groups that are in decline.

Nations, people, the human race are living now in a new world, though their thoughts remain in the old: therein lie humanity's hopes as well as humanity's misfortunes.

PART ONE

THE TWILIGHT OF THE IDEOLOGIES

I

I find it almost impossible to describe the pain and distress I have suffered over the past fifteen years, particularly when I was in prison, as a result of my unsparing efforts to thrash out my ideas—pondering their deeper meaning, their practicability and eventual outcome; thinking about the revolution, its promise and the aftermath, its enthusiasms and betrayals. But no! It was not because I had sacrificed so much of the joy of life, and the literary creativity of my best years, to the teaching of ideas and to the revolution: these have been my greatest joy and my most perfect work. Something else was at stake: nothing less than the continuing existence of myself as myself. Add to this, in the ten years I spent in jail I found no one with whom I could share my doubts and speculations, which, logical yet exanimate, struggled from my desolate brain into the illimitable, inhuman void —into a world of iron bars, walls, warders, and small groups of convicted felons.

To keep me from exerting a bad influence on the other prisoners, so I was told, not without cynicism, by the prison authorities, but actually to keep them from passing on news about me or carrying messages from me, I spent those years cut off from most of the others, in the company of some fifteen old men, of various nationalities and religions, who were serving sentences for murder. In this group there was always one who could more or less read and write. For a time there were a few educated civil servants, party members serving sentences for fraud, and although I had nothing to hide from them, I suspected them of being informants, and in some cases I was undoubtedly right. . . . I received a visit once a month from my wife, Štefanija, and my little boy, Aleksa, each personifying the unfailing regularity and devotion of ones who fight for the existence of their kin in an alienated, dehumanized world. But the officials, with all the zeal of men frightened of being thought sympathetic to heresy and the chief turncoat, saw to it that these visits did not last more than half an hour; so that I was able to exchange only worries and anxieties with my wife and son, empty hopes and interrupted endearments.

The murderers, for the most part vaporing old men, illiterate or barely literate, were the only human creatures with whom I had any contact that was not artificial, but such talk as we could exchange was always about the worries over their homes and their crops and village life, or about the wretched and petty, the everlasting and outrageous misfortunes of daily prison life.

They were all devout men, and I often asked myself: What drives them to a belief in God? Is it possible for men to live without a faith, without some sort of belief, without objectives or ideals? They could not give me an answer, though there were a few honest and sharp-witted ones among them; for the rest, they were stupid, mean, and treacherous men, and, moreover, lust for evil deeds in some had not been quenched by long years of hard labor and languishment. Yet I did learn something from living among them—I the trained atheist who had spared neither kith nor kin, let alone strangers, in my fight for ultimate brotherhood among men. While there was little I could learn from what they had to say, or from their conduct, I felt stimulated when I thought about them as human beings with whom, in spite of the differences in our ways of life, I had become identified, and who seemed to set an irrevocable seal upon my life, in the uneventful and lifeless world of prison. . . . They will remain in my memory as long as it endures and in my writing as long as people find any value in it.

While the younger prisoners were urged to give up their religion, no one, and certainly none of the old men, was forbidden to say his prayers. There was no chaplain or place of worship in the prison, so some people said their prayers in secret, for fear of offending the prison authorities. Others found that spurning secrecy while they prayed was an affirmation of their steadfastness in their faith. Still others made their piety conspicuous, this being the only way they could with impunity defy the godless authorities and the prevailing social order. The nature of the authorities' attitude toward the religious prisoners was expressed one day by a warder who was asked by a demented old man whether it was forbidden to make the sign of the cross: "It's not forbidden," he answered, "but it's not nice." Among these old men there was no solidarity, not even religious solidarity generally speaking. Some of them informed on people whose religious zeal in some completely harmless way contravened the regulations or violated those political doctrines and rules that are unwritten yet somehow known to everyone.

Even so, ill-assorted as they were, envenomed with continual denunciations of each other, and embittered by shattered hopes, they all had an unwavering faith in something good, unsullied, illimitable, of which they themselves were a part by virtue of that essence or aspect of their beings which was also pure, free from offenses, and not subject to life's spoiling. . . . And I had a similar sort of ineffable feeling of belonging to some dateless unrevealed reality, a feeling identified with an inexplicable sense of my own, or, rather, human, invincibility in the clash with the objective world, with the powers and laws governing it. I managed to find an explanation for this realization; and it proved its worth, to me and to others, through beliefs and purposes not to be found among those old convicts, though in essence, in its refusal to submit to harsh realities, in its hope for some future, insubstantial, dateless justice, it was identical with their faith. This realization, this feeling, built up inside me in the desolate life to which I had been condemned by police pressures. It was particularly intense during my twenty months of solitary confinement, when, under tremendous psychological pressure, I felt I was faced with the choice of madness or recantation. I chose madness, and in due course conquered myself, the facts of my life, and the forces that had brought the dilemma upon me. . . . Yes, this realization or feeling gradually bored into my consciousness and honeycombed it. I remember how it all began—the very day, even the hour, perhaps in the same way that converts and anchorites remember the moment when the godhead was revealed to them.

It was on the night of December 7/8, 1953.

Although I had, as usual, fallen asleep about midnight, I woke up suddenly, smitten within by some unfaltering, fateful realization that I would not be able to abandon my views. At that time I had written a series of articles, said by others to be "revisionist," for the party newspaper, *Borba*. I knew that my views were bound to lead me into conflict with my comrades on the Central Committee, men with whom I had burned away my youth and half of my mature years in search of an ideal which, after so many hopes and so much blood and toil, had proved unreal and unrealizable. My wife, Štefanija, was sleeping silently on the far side of the room; but I was aware of her presence in the dark, in the interminable silence of the night. I tried to thrust away my forebodings, obstinate in their insistence that something final had come to pass, something within me, or something affecting me, which meant that I would have to subordinate my way of life, my hopes—and, what is worse, subordinate my family or even sacrifice it altogether. I knew that I had no prospect of winning. I recalled Trotsky's fate and said to myself: Better Trotsky's fate than Stalin's, better to be defeated and destroyed than to betray one's ideal, one's conscience. Even the probable length of a prison sentence (it was usually seven to nine years for "slandering" the state or conducting "hostile propaganda") whirled in my brain, as though it had already been pronounced. I saw myself isolated, with my comrades despising me and slandering me, with my family terrified and at their wit's end; I saw myself among the so-called little people, who would have no way of knowing whether I was a madman or a sage. But the tussle within me was short-lived; it lasted just a few minutes, until I had time to collect my thoughts from sleep and recover from my intimations. Because I already knew, yes *knew,* that this was my true self, and that I could not renounce it, in spite of the vacillations to which I had succumbed, in spite of the more crucial ordeal that I would have to face. I got up and went to my study, and there I jotted down, in a few sentences, what I now knew: the emergence of my differences with the rulers of the party, the inevitability of my parting company with them, the portending trial of my own strength, or my weakness, in deviating from their path. . . . Three weeks later I was officially informed of the proceedings against me by Edvard Kardelj, who until recently had agreed with my criticisms of public policy but was now my prosecutor; and, against my wife's advice, I destroyed my notes, for fear they might fall into the hands of the secret police and be construed to show that I had "consciously planned" in advance to carry out my "antiparty" activity. The truth is that my antidogmatist activity was indeed the result of conscious planning. From the beginning, in spite of the ghastly and bleak resistance to it put up by all my hitherto-held beliefs, by my devotion to my comrades, and by the delights found only in the fruits of power, I had been driven along ineluctably by the forces within me and by the social forces outside me. . . .

After that night I moved gradually but unfalteringly farther away from official dogmas and standpoints, coming into conflict with the actual situation in my own country and inside Communism as a whole, but without admitting to myself or my comrades (and I have not done so to this day) that I had become "anti-Marxist" or "anti-Communist," and least of all that I had turned to the West or to "alien ideologies." The same can be said about my attitude toward religion: in disassociating myself from Marxist dogmatism, I have not turned to any other faith—unless that word can be applied to my firm attachment to the imperative of the human conscience and the inevitability of struggle against tyranny over human existence, to my firm belief in the inseparability of man from the universe, of personal destiny from Mankind's destiny, and in the inexhaustible potentialities of the human mind in spite of, and because of, its alienation from society and from matter. To put it simply, I acted more from conscience than from knowledge or experience. For that reason I was less concerned to compare Marxist theories with the realities of Communist societies than to express my own imaginative pictures and my speculations on such realities. There never has been, and never can be, complete identity between ideas and their eventual materialization, since man is capable only of designing and fighting for his design, unlike God, who creates out of his own mind. I have never at any time wished to retract a single syllable, or to budge an inch, in order to avoid the consequences of what any words or deeds like these may bring in the future. Therefore, I have not referred to my "defection" as a disappointment or a fulfillment, though to me it was both, but, rather, as a creative act—the expression of new ideas, the exploration of new opportunities for my own people and country, for human beings.

If the sacrifice of my way of life to conscience and a preference for ideas rather than realities constitute a faith, then I found mine that night, and, like my comrades in misfortune the old convicts, I have been warmed by it and fortified to overcome vicissitudes and hardships far beyond anything my conscience, and certainly the consciences of my oppressors, could possibly imagine. I mention this as an experience that might be useful to others; but I consider my conduct to have been not heroism but obedience to imperatives that also operate in other people whenever they are trapped in a situation in which they have to fight for their "immortality," for some sort of survival. Among my old convicts it would have been difficult to find anyone who was not prepared to die for his faith; and I, in spite of my fears, doubts, and anxieties, was incapable of acting otherwise than I did, even if I had wanted to.

But creation, although a "godlike act," is a torment

and vexation for the creator himself. For the sake of the ideas, for the sake of the work itself, I had to take account of the facts as they were.

With the victory over Stalin, Tito was elated, but he had already begun to calm down, fearing that the undammed streams might overflow the channels he had built for them, while at the same time the most highly developed and powerful parts of the world were in a spiritual blood feud and aligned in two blocs whose weaponry had assumed cosmic and absurd aspects. The work stoppage in the channel cut through Stalinism seemed to me less a waste of sacrifices and hopes than the loss of the great opportunity to open the gates wider for greater mobility and a freer shaping of society. Nevertheless, within the world's apocalyptic blood brotherhood— in the midst of the Cold War—I did sense a genuine desire for world unity and indeed saw signs of the inevitability of this. And although I felt I was courting incalculable risks of disaster for myself, I knew that Tito was not Stalin—that in Tito's view Stalin's frenzy and dogma were cold calculations and pragmatic policies. I knew Tito's instinctual, ever-vigilant sense of danger, which drove him to impetuosity. But I knew, too, that he was aware of his impetuosity, and that he did not succumb to it when making important political decisions. I felt that Tito would not destroy me, for the simple reason that this would be a "historical error" for him and would magnify the importance of my ideas.

I could not be sure about my speculations. Tito had strengthened his personal power in a party that the struggle with Stalin had turned into an oligarchy. This meant, as far as relationships and concepts in a hitherto Stalinist party were concerned, that it was a more democratic party. The decisive change in Tito's attitude, and in my appreciation of the halt to the democratizing process, came at the plenary session of the Central Committee on the island of Brioni in the summer of 1953. In front of Kardelj and my other comrades I was unable to conceal my disapproval of the decision, against all custom, to assemble the entire Central Committee in Tito's island residence, instead of in its own headquarters in Belgrade; but Kardelj replied that this was of no importance, and the others kept a downcast silence. There was an uneasiness in the atmosphere and the arrangements: there we were, former guerrilla fighters and defenders of the oppressed, in the lap of luxury, but also in a sort of fortress, with a superfluous escort of guards everywhere. And during the actual session, Tito whispered to me significantly, using my familiar nickname: "You will have to speak, Djido, so people won't think we're in disagreement." I was staggered by his manner, and particularly by his oblique insistence that we must be in agreement. I did make a speech, although there was nothing on the agenda that obliged me to speak or touched on my interests. It was the muddled, contradictory speech of a man doing his best to please someone else without being false to himself. Overnight I considered my position, and on the following day, on the road through Lika on our way to fish for trout, I told Kardelj that I would not be able to support the course we were now adopting. He, very wisely, avoided the issue, remarking merely that I was exaggerating what was a transitional stage in "our socialist development," not an essential feature of it. Neither of my two later personal meetings with Tito stopped me from swimming farther upstream. The first of these took place in the autumn of 1953 in the Beli Dvor in Belgrade, at my own request, because I wanted to hear his views on my writing; the second, shortly afterward, at a dinner in my flat arranged by our wives and also attended by Kardelj and Ranković with their wives. At the Beli Dvor meeting Tito said that he liked my writing; but I suspected he did not really mean it—that his mind was not yet made up. And at the dinner in my flat (the only one of its kind to take place in the highest party circle) everything went smoothly but cautiously, as it is apt to with men who have emerged victors after terrible battles and have become wise but careful in their mutual relationships.

And that was how it was with me: I remained uncommitted, of two minds, until the night of December 7/8, 1953. After that night I continued to expound my views, trying to put them into perspective, and I did so with increasing zeal but always trying to ensure that I would not be trapped into harboring a grudge against Tito or any of my comrades on the Central Committee, let alone into starting an intrigue against them—in spite of the void that was beginning to spread around me, in spite of the formality and coolness that had replaced the affectionate greetings of former days, in spite of the snickerings on the side. . . .

And so I made a start, and in my breakthrough to my own view of things I believed that I was right and cared little or not at all whether I was going to win. That is how it was, that is how it is today, and that is how I hope it will always remain. . . .

It is no wonder, with all this, and after being in prison, that I asked myself the question: What connection can my fate and the faith of my old convicts have with the "revelation" that Lenin expounded on the essence of God, one that "happened" neither "in history" nor "in real life"? This is how he expressed it in a letter to Gorki: "God, in history and in real life, is primarily a complex of ideas born of the intolerable oppression of man by the outside natural world and by class enslavement—ideas that reinforce the oppression and mute the class struggle." [1] And here is his "scientific explanation," rebellious, vulgar, and mechanical, of religion: "Religion is one aspect of spiritual enslavement, thrust at all times and in all places upon the masses of the people, who are oppressed by perpetual labor in the service of others and by privations and loneliness. The impotence of the exploited classes in the struggle against their exploiters inevitably gave rise to a belief in a better afterlife, just as the helplessness of savages gave rise to a belief in gods, devils, miracles, and the like." [2]

No faith, and least of all those beliefs of mine that are not greatly concerned either with the practical realities of this world or with the fear of death, is any longer explained satisfactorily to me by Marx—not even in this passage, one of the most profound in his writings: "The religious world is only a reflection of the real world. Take a society of producers of commodities, where the

1. *Sochinenia,* fourth ed., Moscow, 1955, Vol. 35, p. 93.
2. *Ibid.,* Vol. 10, p. 65.

general relationships in production are such that the relation of producers towards their product is that of a relation towards *commodities,* i.e., towards *values,* so that in that material form the producers bring their individual labors into a reciprocal relationship as *undifferentiated human labor.* For a society such as this the most suitable *form of religion is Christianity* with its cult of the abstract man, particularly Christianity in its bourgeois stages of development, its protestantism, deism, and the like. . . . And in general, *the religious reflection* of the real world will not disappear until the relationships between people in their practical everyday life can be seen to have become reasonable everyday relations between man and his fellow man, and between man and nature. The life process in society, i.e., the process of production, will not shed the mystical veil from its face until production has come under the conscious and purposive control of men in free association. This, however, demands a material basis for society, or a series of material conditions for existence, which is itself the spontaneous outcome of a long and painful history of development." [3] But did the faith of my old convicts reflect any reality except their own inner one and that of their forefathers? And is not Catholicism just as appropriate for bourgeois development as Protestantism? And is not Buddhism sometimes (as in Japan, for instance) also "the most suitable" religion for a "society of commodity producers"? And in fact have the relationships in "practical everyday life" under Communism today, where production is under "purposive control," been

3. *Capital,* Belgrade, 1947, Vol. I, p. 43.

"seen to have become" more "reasonable everyday relations between man and his fellow man, and between
man and nature"? Why is it that some religions go on
surviving even though they are no longer a "reflection of
the real world" from which they are supposed to have
originated?

In consciously choosing my own destiny, I discovered,
even before my imprisonment, that my ideas could not
be reduced to a "reflection of the real world"; and my
partnership in suffering with the old convicts compelled
me to be fair to them, and to recognize that the same was
true of their faith.

On going to prison in 1956, I was beginning to think
that the Marxist maxims on the "withering away" of religion were not much more reliable than those on the
"withering away" of the state. But I would not say that
this had any influence either on my conduct or on my
views. As my ideas began to branch out inside me, I
could feel them gaining strength and giving me
strength. At the same time I became an even more confirmed atheist—not for any rational or scientific reasons,
but from purely personal, ideational, and existential
reasons. I was not, nor am I today, one of those Communists who go back to their ancestral religion after having
been disappointed with the realities of Communism, or
who, more difficult still, invent a new religion for themselves. I had not "lost my faith." I had "found" it in the
inexorabilities of broadening the groundwork of the human condition, in visions of change and replacement in
existing societies, in both East and West, because, with

their obsolete dogmas and social patterns, they belong to a bygone age.

And if I sometimes felt at my wit's end, torn by doubts in my "faith" and beset by notions of the existence of some higher law which sets everything in motion, including my personal destiny, I reacted at once against such "culpable" weaknesses and lack of faith. I reveled in the fiendish notion that, if the existence of God should become incontrovertible, I would rebel against his omniscience and immutable order, in the same way that I had reveled in my heretical infection of the party's despotic, inhuman, and contrived unity. Revolt against "higher powers" was to me a sign of man's creative life force no less categorical than his propensity to bow to the inevitable. At that time I had not come across Camus's well-known aphorisms: "Man is the only creature who refuses to be what he is" [4] and "I rebel, therefore we exist";[5] but if I had, I would certainly have included them in my prison notes as an epitome of my own feelings and thoughts.

With all this, I felt a growing respect for the human being, for everything human that was not destructive of the human life force, and consequently of beliefs. Religions, atheism, doctrines, and ideas all appeared before me in my prison solitude, through the prism of my own fate, as unavoidable aspects and diversities of human life, as links between man and the world and between man and his fellow man. I had my being, I held fast to my faith; but hope was not with me. . . .

4. Albert Camus, *L'homme révolté*, Paris, 1951, p. 22.
5. *Ibid.*, p. 36.

I came to this conclusion: in the world of life and society, what men believe is important, because creeds are banners. But at that particular moment what seemed to me more crucial, both for myself and for all who had become disillusioned with Communism, was the answer to these questions: Is it, or is it not, essential for men to have a belief? Is a struggle within Communism possible without ideas or a program? What I have learned and suffered is categorical: a man without a faith, without ideas and ideals, can be imagined only as a man in a world of absolute void—the world of his own nonexistence. And those who maintain that man can be without a faith, without ideas and ideals, are only revealing another aspect of believing—their own. Their own lack of faith is only a particular method of adaptation. I do not dispute or underestimate such views and such a way of life, but I exclude the possibility that they can be of use in bringing change to any society, particularly a rigid and inflexible one such as Communism. Although the arenas depend upon their spectators, it is not the spectators who win the contests.

These confessions and reflections of mine may seem superfluous. But my ideas, in the solitude to which I had been committed, could have had no stronger endorsement than the manner in which they were born.

Another reason this sort of explanation seems to be most feasible is that it was through imprisonment and ordeal, through dejection and exaltation, that I became convinced that no alternative to Communism is to be found in the existing religions or in a new religion. I do not stress this because I fail to see the significance of religions and faiths, and the compelling need for them; nor is it because I have less confidence today in the virtue of my revolt and my ideas—namely, that radical changes in Communism will take place, and are already doing so, principally caused by the system itself, as a result of the unreality of its ideology and the bleak outlook for the future of its reality. It is primarily because of the very nature and mission of religions that I am led to reject the possibility of their playing a revolutionary social role in Communism. Unlike political doctrines, they have no relevance for a specific society or life situation, but are concerned with undifferentiated human destiny and with a moral way of life. Religions inspire and invigorate man above and beyond the potentiality he can find in himself or in the world outside him, but they cannot, in the modern world, change any particular society, because their aims and essence stretch above and beyond every society. They are unsuitable as alternatives to a particular Communist system because the people living under that system are exhausted and sated, as things stand, with all kinds of revelations and governing laws—all of them "ultimate" and "scientific." Since Communism is changing on its own—through what democratic Communists and socialists are learning and doing—the criticism and ideas that will change it must possess a new, a real and more credible scientific character than its own ideology. Awareness is essential for the societies in which we live; for a long time to come, Communists will be obsessed with "science" and the "scientific." The same is true of Communist socialism: it becomes viable, *i.e.*, democratic, only if stripped of Marxist dogmas like "leadership for action," which means privileges and powers based on ideological allegiance. Communism's ability to construct a scientific ideology as an exclusive body of knowledge about the world and man, and hence as a substitute for religion, has proved limited, so that it has now turned into a body of colorless, muscle-bound dogmas. But this condition does not in itself provide the religions with any special opportunities, except that under the new conditions they will find new opportunities for asserting themselves. The yearning for the Kingdom of Heaven is indestructible in man, but it cannot be a substitute for practicable, political, intellectual, and economic freedom for men who are toil-worn and have been driven frantic by Communism's policy of violent aggrandizement.

Religions have, it is true, survived under Communism and are proving that they can outlast it, but they have not contributed any real criticism either of its ideology or of its practical aspects. This is not owing to weakness or error; it is just that it is not in their nature to do this, and they have not yet stretched their capabilities.

But there are exceptions to every "rule": some churches have taken an interest in social affairs, some more and some less; and there are some, even today, that are in control of political parties. The question is whether religion in its political and social activities will be permitted to play a greater or lesser ideological role; in the Middle Ages it was a particularly significant role, and may well be so again in the future. When Communism has come to power in Catholic countries, it has failed conspicuously in its attempts to deprive the church and religion of this aspect of their activities. So it is not altogether out of the question, particularly in one of these Catholic countries, that a movement might base its ideology on religion and construct a more or less successful program of political action. These circumstances are probably owing to the international character of the Catholic church and, equally, to the attention it pays to the course of events and to adapting itself to the world as it is. Although I do not deny the possibility of such movements, I do not believe that they and only they are capable of understanding and embracing all the new, diverse and complex, conceptual and factual, problems introduced and imposed by Communism.

The evidence is that society itself passes into stagnation and illiberality once the conscience of its individual members—religion, in other words—comes under the control of monopolistic ideologies, with church and state constantly sparring for supremacy. Church leadership can never be the same thing as political leadership, nor can the transformation of society be carried out without clear, thoroughly worked out, practicable programs. For good or ill, that is how it has always been, and it cannot be otherwise so long as human beings remain as they are. Freedom has bounds; but it cannot become a piece of property. Any attempt to appropriate freedom for a particular doctrine or social group can only result in loss of freedom for them, too.

Such reflections have been occasioned by the present state of relations between religion and Communism. Right up to the time the Communists directed their efforts toward an ultimate objective, in effect a religious one, they had been unable to find a common language with religion. The language they employ with religion today, however, is one in which they renounce (albeit tacitly) their ideal objectives: their dogmatic ideas and their monolithic aspects are disguised by empirical and pragmatic ideas and by practicable, accessible programs very much the same as those of any other political party anywhere else in the world.

Communism has not only failed to become a religion, a "scientific" one, in fact, but it has also disintegrated as a world ideology. Perhaps more significantly, it is disintegrating as a monopolistic national one. The Communist parties of the future will have no alternative but to be, at the very best, what in fact they are: sociopolitical movements that strive in collaboration with others to achieve certain definite patterns of society and government under their own national conditions.

II

The past becomes a living reality as soon as we begin
to investigate and inquire into it, so that it can never be
revealed in all its diversity even if the investigator were
to be stripped of all personal bias. Marx's place in history is difficult to determine because his doctrine is
more than a mere presence; in one way or another it is
active and fermenting, emerging from all the vent holes
of contemporary history. But I am not taking the historian's approach, because I am not a historian; nor do
I take the approach of those angry detractors of his doctrine who have suffered from its application. I approach
it as one who was until recently one of his disciples and
who came to realize, through the ordeals suffered by his
country and through his own personal experiences, that
Marx's ideas were unrealizable. Today I think I can, in all
good conscience, expound my view, incomplete though
it may be, of Marx and the historical role of his doctrine.

Like every other work of genius, Marx's is a synthesis:
his doctrine linked and made new uses of British political economy (Smith, Ricardo), French socialism (Saint-

Simon and, latently, Fourier), and German philosophy (Kant, Hegel, Feuerbach). These were not the only streams of contemporary European thought to serve as a source for his views, but they were the most important. They are blended with the findings of other thinkers and scientists, some of whom, though less significant than the ones mentioned, did stimulate Marx's imagination to original and far-reaching generalizations. Mignet, with his interpretation of the French Revolution as a class struggle, is an example. In this connection, it seems to me that too little stress has been laid upon the ideas that Marx borrowed from Spinoza. Marx incontrovertibly owed Spinoza in making the identification of freedom with necessity. He probably was influenced, too, by the concept of the Absolute, which for Spinoza was God, and for Marx was matter. Marx came from a German Jewish family converted to Protestantism. It would be very speculative, however, to maintain that this dualism in his own life—a commitment to Judaism coexisting with Germanism—influenced his alignment and visions of the future. But there is no doubt that at the beginning of his intellectual activity (*A Contribution to the Jewish Question,* in 1844, for example) he presented himself as one of those Jews who had suffered because of their origins and for that reason bore, with the overmastering fervor of a people under a curse, witness to the highest values in Judaism and in the Jews themselves. Since his image today is primarily that of a prophet, it seems to me that his roots go right back to the Bible—to the inexorable destiny that the ancient prophets revealed to the "chosen people," and through them to the whole human race.

Yet no greater injustice could be done to Marx than to examine his thought piecemeal and in isolation from its whole; this kind of fallacious approach could even prove that there is nothing very original in Shakespeare or in Aristotle. Marx, in fact, is one of those rare beings who epitomize in themselves whole epochs and, to paraphrase T. S. Eliot, compel all previous values to make room for them and to be measured by them. With a versatility that defies analysis, Marx, I would say, was a powerful combination of three characteristics, which give his works as a whole their remarkable unity: he was at once a prophet, a scientist, and a writer.

Marx himself would probably have poured scorn on anyone who remarked on his prophetic propensities. For if it is hard to be a prophet in one's own country, it is harder still for the prophet, at the moment of his utterances, to know whether he is a prophet or not. Nevertheless, in these latter days, Marx can be seen not only as a prophet, but, indeed, as the first prophet of world importance and stature, because he wrote in the age of world-wide communication. Like earlier prophets, he uttered his prophecies with poetic power and expounded them with the persistence and conviction of one who believes he has discovered the higher, ultimate truth.

The age of Marx saw peasant and craft trading being rapidly transformed into a planned industry that was advancing with the aid of scientific technology. It was an age that abounded in prophets, particularly because the radical changes taking place in European society stirred thinkers to recognize the dire poverty and brutality about them and the uprooting of peasants and craftsmen from their centuries-old ways of life and familiar ways of thinking. But none of these prophets possessed Marx's many-sided, synthesizing brain, and none of them believed so wholeheartedly in the power of science or used the scientific method so much as did Marx. All the nineteenth-century prophets, apart from Marx, failed to understand, because they were incapable of understanding, that all nations, the entire population of the globe, must perforce change, and keep changing, their ways of life, which means that they must also change their social relationships, adapting them to the improvements in industry.

If prophecy is merely foreseeing the inevitable, then Marx was the farthest-seeing prophet into the industrialized way of life, into the abolition of distinctions between mental and manual work, and into the productive intercommunication of the human race. But he, like every other prophet, was mistaken as regards the concrete methods and forces needed to bring all this about. Although it can be said that he foresaw that these changes would destroy entrenched property relationships, he did not predict the new social patterns that would then emerge. Private property is no longer sacrosanct in the societies that were subjected to his merciless criticism, whereas the new societies inspired by his views are quite different from what he imagined they would be.

Of all modern prophets, Marx made the most consistent approach to society as an object of scientific investigation, thus becoming the founder of modern social science—or sociology. Although there were other theorists engaged in this field, pre-eminence here does not fall upon either Auguste Comte or Herbert Spencer, because Comte engaged more in speculation about society than in research into it and because his conclusions are tinged with mysticism, while even if Spencer had possessed Marx's profundity and breadth of vision, the simple truth is that his social studies were in fact published after Marx's. It is important for people active in politics and the realm of ideas to know which of Marx's conclusions have proved accurate and which inaccurate; yet it is essential to recognize that in the history of science and human thought he was the first to realize that it is possible to *investigate* society, just as it is any other phenomenon. In *Capital* he set about investigating one of its aspects, capitalism, first and foremost English capitalism.

As for Marx as a writer, although his great qualities were recognized during his lifetime, they have received only the scantiest analytical attention. I cannot dwell upon them here, for reasons of space and because my purpose is different, but I would draw attention to the baroque splendor of his style, the liveliness and breadth of his associations, the heights of his humor, and his prodigious gift of giving sparkle to the dullest data and most trivial situations. Marx's descriptions of the proletariat's grinding poverty and hand-to-mouth existence, of the greed and inhumanity of the capitalists, at the beginning of the nineteenth century, are among the most shattering documents ever written, the most agonizing pictures ever conjured up; and his analyses of the political struggles in France, particularly during the reign of Louis Napoleon, are among the most lively and authentic pictures of historical events ever drawn. In reading Marx one can almost hear the roar, as tumultuous as Homeric battles, of implacable multitudes seeking unremitting retribution. In his visions of the future one can sense, as in the frenzied acting out of destiny in a play by Sophocles, the forceful changing of whole societies for the sake of a new prospect, because of a fateful destiny—for Marx, the imperishable, everlasting dream of brotherhood and equality among men.

These qualities, quite apart from the world-wide influence of his ideas, place Marx among the most portentous minds in human history, and they ensure his presence will never be forgotten, even after his doctrine has lost ground and become inert in society.

None of Marx's collaborators and disciples matched his beauty of style, his depth of thought, and, most of all, his versatility. This can be said even in face of the fact that there have been revolutionaries among them, like Lenin and Mao Tse-tung, who have shaken the whole globe, and leaders among them, like Stalin, who have masterminded the shaping of international relations. The creativeness of all of these men, indeed, expressed itself in their grasp of the revolutionary essence of Marx's teaching, while to a large extent each ignored its integrality and each developed that aspect of it which in practice is the only one to have proved itself. For Lenin this aspect was the party and revolution; for Stalin it was the state machinery and industrialization; for Mao Tse-tung it was guerrilla warfare and the systematic organization of the masses, and for all of them it was the industrial transformation of society by means of dictatorship.

The fate of Marxist ideology, and of Communism as a social system, is different from what Marx and his disciples conceived. The question posed by the Cold War was: Is the whole world going to go Communist? But the disintegration of international Communism into national states and parties, with the two Communist superpowers scrambling for them, finally exposed the absurdity of the question. Variety is the essence of people and nations, and for a long time now Communism has not been identical everywhere in actual practice, nor has it even represented the same idea. The revision of ideology and practice is still carried out in the Communist world in the name of the "purity of the faith," so no one need be impressed by the declarations of loyalty to Marxism sworn by all the Communist leaderships. The patterns of national life are becoming increasingly varied, so that today such declarations are being made as some leaders are in fact abandoning an unsuitable ideology rather than remaining faithful to it. The question of Communism's conquest of the world is no longer posed by anyone but the Chinese leaders, and the reason is that their country, still in a strait jacket after the throes of its own revolution, is deceiving itself and others that the same thing is happening all over the world.

The relevant question today is the fate of Marxist ideology, and consequently of Communism, as a social system. This is not a question that has arisen out of the Cold War, nor has it been imposed by sundry "bourgeois" outlooks, in other words by "the imperialists," as Soviet propagandists like to maintain. Rather, it has been imposed by the breakup and plight of Marxist ideology itself. The fate of Marxism is being determined, in fact, by the change in Communist societies themselves —in the realities that are justified and inspired by Marxism. The theory and practice of Communism have always been closely associated. Marxist ideology has offered a sufficiency of sophisticated and utopian formulas for the vindication of Communist action, but the action or practice is too coercive to maintain the power and the glory of the ideology. Now that the unity of Communist societies has been irremediably and irrevocably broken up, Communism in practice is ceasing to be Communist, and it finds itself increasingly less capable of being so— of being, that is, a bureaucratic party monopoly over the economy, the state, and thought. But as a state is inconceivable without ideas and ideational models, there is posed with great urgency this question: What is going to happen to Communist, or, rather, Marxist, ideology and what is going to replace it?

The East European Communist parties—and, in a different way, the West European Communist parties— faced with the actual situation of the contemporary world have three possible answers to this question thrust before them: first, the eventuality that Marxism will survive as a monolithic and monopolistic ideology; second, the possibilities of a renascence and rejuvenation of Marxism; third, the possibilities of a survival of Marxism

48

alongside other ideas—so-called ideological coexistence for countries under Communism.

The course of events has already traced the answer to the first alternative: international Communism has long been fragmented into national movements, and some of these are more or less independent of the two disparate and opposed Communist world powers, the Soviet Union and China. Those who have taken the view that Communism as an all-binding world ideology reached the limit of its expansion under Stalin have been proven right, and it must be admitted that then it was wearing its most sinister, inhuman, and tyrannical aspects. After Stalin's death, the modification of Marxism, whether in the Khrushchev revised version or in Mao Tse-tung's dogmatic one, resulted in no substantial gains as regards either expanding the movement or developing the theory; and the reason is that the existence of two centers, Moscow and Peking, each wrangling for hegemony over the "outside" movements, was bound to jeopardize the orthodoxy of both. Nearly all new developments in Communism today are taking place in national Communist movements and by means of their mutual relationships. Unity of the world Communist movement is today unthinkable, even if China and the Soviet Union were to find a common language, and for that to happen they would have to cease existing as two separate great powers. Moreover, the unrest of East European states under Soviet domination is obvious, and no one should be surprised by a split between Hanoi and China when Vietnam becomes united under the Hanoi government.

In accord with the terms of the Marxian legacy, Communists consider nationalism as the deadliest sin, yet the irony is that, with the passing of time, nationalism has imposed itself as the surest way for Communists to get to enjoy the fruits of power—that greatest of all delights. But the damnation and the delight of this sin know no bounds. We are now living in a period of disintegration in the systems of national Communism, the disintegration of Marxism-Leninism as a monolithic and monopolistic ideology on a *national* basis.

This means that we have passed to the second possible answer to the question of the future of Marxism: its possibilities for renascence and rejuvenation.

The disintegration of Communist ideology, and thus the change in the practice of Communism, is taking place slowly in particular areas of national life. Apart from China, Cuba, and Albania, and to some extent the Soviet Union, the coercion of art for the momentary requirements of the party or to comply with resurrected dogmas has fallen into disuse or been abandoned in all Communist countries, and in some of them (Czechoslovakia, Poland, and Yugoslavia, for example) the interpretation and development of Marxist philosophy and of sociology are no longer the chief concern of party forums and of officials superficially "charged" with this duty. These disciplines are now in the more-or-less free and critical hands of philosophers and scientists.

Writers and artists have taken foremost places among those devoting their creative activities to destroying rigid formulas and attitudes, and they were the first to set about a spontaneous demolition of Stalin's and Lenin's (and indeed other Marxist) dogmas; but now this has become the thoughtful and creative work of philosophers, sociologists, and historians. From the ruins of Stalinist dogmatism in Eastern Europe unofficial Marxist theoreticians have been springing up in their tens and their hundreds. Some of them, like Professor Georgy Lukacs in Hungary, with his devastating criticism of Stalinism as "thought without meditation," have opened the door to a new approach to Marxism itself. Others, like Professor Leszek Kolakowski, in Poland, Karel Kosik, in Czechoslovakia, and Gajo Petrović and Mihailo Marković, in Yugoslavia, have already reached an "open Marxism" in their criticism, a Marxism that is not monopolistic but is regarded as viable in confrontations with other theories and views.

Within the Soviet Union, however, Marxist thinking is still held by the strait jacket of the party bureaucracy and is obsessed by the leading world role of the Soviet state, so that it has not gone much beyond the bounds of the official criticism of Stalin. Marxists in other East European countries have gone beyond "national" Communism, *i.e.*, further than mere resistance to Moscow and to Leninist dogmatism. But the same cannot be said of the national party bureaucracies; although all their pores are suppurating with unbelief, they fear for their own monopolistic grip on the levers of power, and they have had neither the courage nor the strength to break out of the vicious circle of party unity, though this is only illusory, and of ideological monopoly, though this is only verbal. So far, only the free-minded intellectuals and democratic Communists of the developed and traditionally democratic state of Czechoslovakia have sought to pass the bounds of the national party bureaucracy and to seize the opportunities offered, and they made their attempt through allowing a freedom of the press, that thorn in the flesh of all party bosses and East European bureaucrats. It seems obvious that socialism can survive such attempts, if socialism is not taken to mean monopoly by the party bureaucracy. It was the *party bureaucracy* in the Soviet Union that was exceedingly disturbed, as much from fear of the "Czech plague," as for their own imperial interests.

The developments in Czechoslovakia provide evidence that events will lead, not toward a renascence of Marxism, but toward its decline as a monopolistic ideology, toward all sorts of variations of Marxism, with other ideas arising and thriving by the side of Marxist ones.

Communist parties are not being transformed into purer, more Marxist and revolutionary parties; they are becoming, however slowly and despite setbacks, ideologically disunited and therefore more democratic, while the society they still dominate is becoming a democratic, stratified society. . . . And so, even if I had not been in prison at the time, I could not have helped regarding the black Soviet clouds that eclipsed the dawn of freedom in Hungary, and the execution of Imre Nagy, as a personal tragedy for myself; while the brief, still unfinished, penetration of the opaque, malign darkness in Czechoslovakia seemed all the more promising for my personal hopes, because I am, at the time, out of prison. I say this even though I did not, and could not, have had any direct contact with events in these two countries. . . .

But how far can the "restorers" of Marxism go in their

criticism of state affairs? What are the possibilities and prospects for such criticism? A consideration of this question will also throw some light on the possibility of a renascence of Marxism. The question applies only within a national framework.

National shortcomings in instigating a renascence of Marxism show that these are not in themselves the real problem. What is at essence is the matter of looking for solutions to the intellectual and economic stagnation so common in various Communist countries. Within these purely national frameworks the possibilities for a national Marxism do not appear to have been completely exhausted, in either West or East European countries. This is true for the lesser Western parties as well, for the Italian and French parties, because exceedingly powerful currents sweep them away from Marxist dogmatism as they liberate themselves from the influence of the Communist great powers and stop paying tribute to the chimera of internationalism. In Yugoslavia the Marxists connected with the magazine *Praxis* succeeded in preserving their independent thinking and keeping official interference at bay; and by criticizing the party bureaucracy's Marxism (a Marxism even more boastful than ignorant, by the way), they have indirectly influenced political developments. On the other hand, the student unrest in Poland, in March 1968, showed that, although the Marxism of Gomulka's party bureaucracy started off as national Communism, it is no longer capable of extricating the party and the country from Moscow's hegemony.

A renascence of Marxism, the dream of Marxist professors and their main preoccupation, is usually the frustrated expression of efforts toward humanizing and democratizing relationships in Communism itself—of transforming despotic forms of government and unfree forms of ownership. These efforts usually involve a return to the sources of Marxism, even to the young Marx, who was still in the shadows of the Hegelian categories and for that reason untainted by the later political and practical needs of the political movement he initiated. Even so, the efforts are basically dogmatic, aimed at a society that will be driven toward the "original," "uncorrupted" idea, *i.e.*, toward a utopia where men would not be "alienated," since there would be no state, no politics, but, rather, only the practice of the principle "From each according to his abilities, to each according to his needs."

This "regeneration" of a Communism in real life that is in fact absurd, unenlightened, and not in the least ideal must appear to be idealistic, academic, and logical. In order to make it more digestible, its proponents today most frequently refer back to Marx's doctrine of alienation. This doctrine was formulated by him at the age of twenty-five and is mainly to be found in the *Economic and Philosophic Manuscripts of 1844,* which were not published until 1932. The ideas here and more particularly his manner of expressing them are recognizable as having just emerged from the shell of neo-Hegelianism. The very notion of alienation was taken by Marx from idealist philosophy, first and foremost from Hegel's, where the basic process of the idea unfolds with its estrangement from itself in various aspects—nature, society, and so on. Although Marx elaborated and augmented his theory of human alienation in *Capital* (in the chapter "The Commodity," particularly in the section "The Fetishistic Character of the Commodity and Its Secret"), the "regenerators" of Marxism and Communism mainly refer back to his youthful exposition, which argues that as private ownership alienates the worker from his product, so it alienates man from man. Without launching into a refutation or endorsement of this doctrine, which is pressed into a mold of dialectical contradictions but is nevertheless inspired with genuine humanism, I can say that Marx here, as in many of his other assumptions, reveals one truth about man—his irresistible compulsion as a rational being to alienate himself from the world and to compensate for that alienation by his own creative activity—a truth that Marx reduces to its one historical form, this being the commodity mode of production. Following in Marx's footsteps, the resurrectionists of infallible Communism fell into the same dialectical trap of identifying the historical form with the timeless content, thus coming to the conclusion that the worker's alienation, an incontrovertible fact in Communist as well as capitalist systems, can be transformed ultimately into freedom by abolishing the intermediary between producer and product; as though this could possibly be carried out without reverting to primitive "commerce," as though man as a being could possibly accept it without renouncing his intellect and consenting to the extinction of his species.

This return to the early Marx is tantamount to an alienation of the real, complete Marx from himself. For what is left of Marx and Communism if they can be rescued and restored only by Marx's doctrine of alienation—certainly the most humanitarian of doctrines, but surely also the most utopian? Why not, then, be consistent and return to Hegel, whose sense of alienation was more original, better elaborated, and perhaps more profound? Or to the myth of the primal state of innocence? But that would be conversion to idealism and religion, from which the "restorers" of Marxism shrink as from the direst treachery. Without questioning the integrity of their viewpoint, one is bound to wonder whether their efforts are less an expression of a new vision and of the real needs of society than of aborted ideals and temporary helplessness.

The question of the renascence of Marxism is not in fact so much a matter of theory as of practical development. Most of the protagonists of this renascence are aware of this, though they fail to realize that to carry it out would require nothing more or less than a new Communist revolution, and that there would be no greater guarantee for its "purity," even with strong supporting trends in society, than there was for the revolutions that have already come to an end in such an impure state.

The opportunities for a Marxist renascence are at hand and limited, as is the national Communism on whose soil they have sprung up. In the same way that national Communism has been able to break away from the orthodox hegemonic center, while failing to adapt national life and the national economy to wider communities and to the demands of modern technology, so the "evolution" and "restoration" of Marxism based on national soil and launched from national perspectives do not seem capable of producing any real and consistent criticism either of Marxist dogmatism or of Communism in practice.

The internal critics of Communism include among their numbers brilliant writers capable of substantiating their views. I do not mean to imply that some of them may not, in the course of change in the actual state of affairs in which they live, make important contributions to and further advances of philosophical thought and society. But that society will not be the one they wanted to restore to the pure idea, and to model on that idea. I believe that they will salvage from Marxism only what is undogmatic and therefore most enduring—a critical attitude toward society, toward its myths, no less than toward its realities. In this society, which has already come into existence, the dialectic will survive and hold its ground, though not as a science or scientific method, because it is neither, but, rather, as it was developed in ancient Greece, as a technique of argument for demonstrating irreconcilable and unimpeachable thinking. . . . The world is satiated with dogmas, but people are hungry for life. . . .

To the third alternative question on the fate of Marxism—what are the prospects for its coexistence with other doctrines?—such experiences as there have been of Communism in practice have so far given a negative answer. The outlook here, however, is no longer completely bleak. Having been a rigid and inflexible revolutionary doctrine in the age of industrialization, Marxism as a comprehensive view of the world, as an ideology, has proved incapable of and unamenable to engaging in open and free coexistence. At first, in its early days, it was its claim to be all-embracing, to be a universal method and theory, that gave it its advantage over other revolutionary doctrines; but in ordinary, nonrevolutionary human situations—particularly after revolution had made it the ideology of a privileged, all-inclusive authority—it became an all-besetting obstacle to other teachings, to new ideas and consequently to freedom of thought. That is why other teachings have usually had no choice but to take root in Marxism itself, like a heresy, achieving their right to live in moments of its weakness, or thanks to the "generosity" and ignorance of the high priests of Marxism. Such teachings have taken root—and now they cannot be eradicated.

Any forms of freedom under Communism are bound to mean an end to the supremacy of Marxism as an ideology. But just as the termination of the Communist power monopoly does not mean destruction of the economic and other foundations laid down during its reign, but is actually a prerequisite for their greater freedom of mobility, so the disintegration and dethronement of Marxist ideology need not, and probably will not, involve the extinction of all Marx's teaching, his ideas and visionary insights. Marx's thoughts, like anyone else's, can only establish their real measure and true worth when emancipated from their idealized form and stripped of their mystique, *i.e.*, in the renunciation and dissolution of the ideology behind them.

A young friend of mine once told me that my prediction of the twilight of the ideologies was what had most impressed him in *The New Class,* and it is to this remark of his that I owe the title of this first section of the book. It is of the utmost importance to stress here that the twilight of the ideologies, and first and foremost of Marxism as being the only real world ideology, does not mean the end of ideas, but, on the contrary, is the prerequisite for their insemination and luxuriant growth. . . . Out of the twilight and from the ruins of ideologies an unconstrained life can come into the world.

III

Marxism is the first real world ideology—*i.e.,* one that has convulsed the whole human race in one way or another. This does not mean that similar objectives have not been pursued before, for, of course, they have: by philosophies, unsuccessfully; and by some religious movements, successfully.

Particularly outstanding and instructive among such attempts are the doctrines and objectives of Plato as set out in his *Republic.* Here for the first time in European philosophy we find a detailed exposition of the ideal state, Plato's own kind of (aristocratic) communist state. It is interesting to note that Plato's attempts to put his teachings into practice in Syracuse, under Dion and Tyrant Dionysius II, ended in disaster, and placed his own life in jeopardy. The essence of Plato's teaching is that philosophers must be at the head of the state, since they are more likely to possess qualities of statesmanship, which are acquired by learning and consist in a knowledge of the absolute values embodied in the machinery of the universe itself. Later, in *The Laws,* Plato, presumably having learned his lesson, abandoned, though not without regret, his ideal communist society as being unsuitable for ordinary men; and the reason people today still turn back to his *Republic* is that Plato's philosophy in its most complete and congruous form is to be found in that work.

There are certain superficial and inverted similarities between the Marxian and Platonic doctrines. Plato outlined his knowledge of society from what he called Forms; and the rule of the philosophers, who were most closely in touch with the transcendental value of the Good, was to be carried out in accord with these Forms. Marx, on the other hand, took his ideas of the ideal society from the laws of its development, *i.e.*, from historical necessity, so the essential for his construction was a knowledge of these social laws. For Plato, the philosopher was the living law; for the Communists, the party is. In spite of these similarities, Marx appears to have had little regard for Plato. As for Lenin, since he considered the development of philosophy as "a struggle between idealism and materialism," [1] "a struggle of parties," [2] he must have felt an instinctive resentment against the progenitor of idealism. For Plato's disciple Aristotle, however, Marx had such a high regard that he almost thought of him as his far-distant teacher. Indeed, Marx, like Aristotle, was as much a scientist as a philosopher; and the similarities in their methodology and in the exhaustiveness of their treatment of any subject undertaken are all too obvious. But there are fundamen-

1. *Materialism and Empirio-criticism*, Belgrade, 1948, p. 375.
2. *Ibid.*, p. 128.

tal differences between them: Aristotle did not approach his researches with any presumptive belief in, or theory about, the inevitability of a more and more improved society, then finally a truly perfect one, and was not in a position to be involved in a struggle over this. As a result, in contradistinction to Plato and Marx, Aristotle in his *Politics* neither described nor expounded any ideal society, but merely analyzed those societies in the real world, showing preference for one or another according to the conditions under which they existed and the human needs that had to be satisfied. That is why no one in history has ever remotely considered constructing a government and society on the basis of Aristotle's theories, although every socialist, even every statesman, can find in them, to this day, imperishable wisdom and enlightenment.

There may be an objection here that it is unnatural, certainly premature, to compare Marx with the two greatest minds of the ancient world. But it was not my intention to draw comparisons, because these thinkers are quite different, and, further, the role and greatness of great men cannot be subjected to comparisons, since each of them is great according to the way he has resolved the problems imposed upon him by the realities and needs of the world.

Nevertheless, the comparison was not accidental: I wish to draw from it the conclusion that, although Marx came nearer to the philosopher-scientist Aristotle, as far as his outlook and method were concerned, Marx's visions of society had more in common with those of Plato, who was not merely a metaphysician and logician but also a mystic and utopian. The differences in the practical consequences resulting from Plato's and Marx's social theories are owing partly to circumstances but primarily to the differences in their approach to their researches: Plato arrived at his ideal society by way of contemplation, extracting it from transcendental ideas (his Forms), while Marx confined his meditations to historical realities, and it was in them that he sought the conditions for his ideal, "classless" society. Plato's deductions were drawn from his hypothetical Forms, which were assumed to be realizable because of their perfection and because matter was "formed" according to their pattern, while Marx's ideas, or one aspect of them at least, derive from his researches into actual social forces and movements in production. So the fact that Marx's ideal society, like Plato's, never came into being, or had the remotest chance of doing so, cannot cancel the enormous difference between the consequences of their social theories. Marx's theories have brought changes to society on a tremendous scale, though in different places and in different ways than he had predicted, while Plato's influence has mainly been in the realm of thought and religion. Marx's scientific approach (unlike Aristotle's) was visionary and resembled a religion in that it motivated hundreds of millions of people—and continues to do so —while Plato's ideal state, precisely because it was logical and metaphysical, has never advanced in practice beyond his abortive experiments in Syracuse. It is quite irrelevant, here, that Marx was an atheist and that Plato was an idealist and mystic. Marx, with his proofs of the inevitability of the new society, was akin to the great prophets; Plato's rational society was unreal, but his philosophy was to serve several centuries later a purpose beyond his imagining. Plato inspired the plans of the early Christian thinker Origen for grounding the newborn religion.

As can be seen from these comparisons, and as will be explained in detail later, there is some common ground between certain aspects of Marx's views, the dialectic in particular, and idealist philosophy, and also between his ultimate objective, the perfect Communist society, and the eschatologies of religion, which is to say, doctrines on the Last Things, like Judgment Day, the Kingdom of Heaven, and so on. Marx's final objective was, however, nearer to that of the utopians Thomas More and Tommaso Campanella, and nearer still to that of the socialist utopians Saint-Simon, N. G. Chernyshevsky, Fourier, and Robert Owen. The same can be said about Marx and the anarchists, like Bakunin: their ultimate objectives were identical, except perhaps that the anarchist one was even more idealistic. But Marx was kept at a distance from all these ideas by the realistic side of his doctrine, which was concerned with discovering practicable lines of action and conditions, or, as he would have put it, the "laws governing the changes in society." Particularly important was his understanding of the social forces in which his ideas were to be embedded. Marx's objective, although its close connection with earthly life differentiates it from the objectives of religion, is by virtue of its *finality* a religious one, and it has made itself felt in history as a utopian one. Though it may have been unattainable as far as the countries where his idea took hold and as far as prevailing conditions and available means were concerned, the plans he mapped for achieving his objective were, in broad outline, shown to be feasible and realizable. If Marx's researches and conclusions had not become identified with the program-planning needs of certain specific social forces and with their faith in redemption, the effect would have been no greater than that of other utopias—although Marx would still occupy the important place that belongs to him as a scientist and writer, but without the revolutionary label attached to his name.

This is certainly so, because the success of ideas in taking root in society and becoming a driving force for men and history does not depend upon their form, upon how scientific they may be; it depends upon the degree to which they are capable of elucidating and motivating the vital aspirations of individuals and social groups. There is no other explanation for the revolutionary role played in history by diverse, even antagonistic, ideas, including religions in the wider sense. The Puritan Revolution in England was carried out in the name of Anglican Puritanism and the Bible. Cromwell stated its ideational and real aspect with brilliant simplicity when he allegedly advised his soldiers to trust in God and keep their powder dry. The French rationalists and materialists were in no way less scientific in the eighteenth century than Marx was in the nineteenth, or than Lenin was at the beginning of the twentieth, and while the society that emerged in the full flush of their ideas was certainly different from the previous one, it was not a whit more "rational" or "enlightened." Rousseau did not preach revolution, nor did he attack religious prejudice, but he experienced and castigated social evils with such passion that he insinuated the desire for social transformation more urgently and more "dangerously" into human minds than most philosophers have. Camus has observed the following: "It is clear that with the *Social Contract* [Rousseau's book] we are present at the birth of a new mystique, because the general will [3] is postulated as God himself. 'Each of us,' says Rousseau, 'places his personality and his entire capabilities under the supreme command of the general will, and we all adopt each individual member as a part of the indivisible whole.' This political entity, having become sovereign, is also defined as a divine entity. It is infallible. . . . 'Under the law of reason, nothing is done without cause.' It is completely free. . . . It is also inalienable and indivisible, and, above all, its aim is to resolve the great theological problem—the contradiction between absolute power and divine innocence. . . . If man is by nature good, if nature as expressed in him is identified with reason, he will display the crowning glory of reason under the sole condition that he is expressing himself freely and naturally. So he can no longer go back on his decision, as from now on it overshadows him. The general will [Marx would say "class" or "class interest"] is primarily the expression of universal reason, which is categorical. [Marx would say

3. "*La volonté générale*," Diderot's phrase, as used by Rousseau, means: since "the good" is identical for all rational beings, real individual personalities will always be identical, so that it can be said that the state, *i.e.*, society, will have a single general will.

66

"the mode of production," which is also categorical.]
The New God is born." [4]

According to this, Marxism and Communism are no
more similar or dissimilar to religion than are any other
ideologies and movements that have set themselves ultimate ideal objectives. *Mutatis mutandis,* this applies to
both Communist revolutions and Communist social systems: they achieved what was socially and historically
possible, not what they invented; and in that respect they
are characteristically as realistic or utopian as the societies and revolutions before them.

But this partial, and perhaps quite illusory, affinity
between religion on the one hand and, on the other,
philosophical systems and closed ideologies—in our time,
Marxism and Communism—may for the latter be a
source of both strength and weakness. In brief, the
strength lies in the vitality, the "this-worldliness," of the
ideal objectives of the ideology with which the masses
are rallied. But since life sooner or later reveals the impossibility of achieving the ideal objectives of ideologies,
they finally become illusions and masks for the unideal,
the ugly, and the intolerable social conditions and forces
that grow in their wake. The same can be said of religions, insofar as they have an ideological side to them;
and this is almost inevitable, since they are represented
by transient, imperfect men living in transient, imperfect conditions. But the fact that religions do not,
in most cases, persistently concern themselves with
"worldly," "ultimate," and nonethical objectives, if they

4. *L'homme révolté,* pp. 147–148.

67

express or represent such things at all, makes them longer-lasting than ideologies and philosophies, and capable of surviving centuries. By this means, in part, religions survive social systems and conditions quite different from those in which they first appeared.

IV

Albert Einstein, that modest, kindhearted professor, took a lively interest in political events, considered himself a socialist, and had sympathy for the sufferings and struggles of the Soviet peoples; yet surely it never entered his head that his calculations and formulas might, however indirectly, shake the foundations of a doctrine that not only claimed to explain the world and bring ultimate happiness to the human race, but also held sway over a considerable area of the earth. But then, neither was it Nicolaus Copernicus' intention that his heliocentric system should shake the foundations of medieval Scholasticism. Although the symbols change and the actors may be different, history repeats itself. It is not chance that in the first country where Communism triumphed, the Soviet Union, Einstein's vision of the world was to have its persecutors and its martyrs.

It is now known that Stalin personally initiated a refutation of Einstein's theory of relativity. He made professional philosophers and scientists capitulate to his demands and formulate his dogmas. Although Stalin knew nothing about modern physics or astronomy, he had that instinctual sense of danger with which founders of despotisms and empires are so richly endowed. In the relativist, unpatterned, and undefinitive picture of order in the universe that emerged from modern physics he sensed a mortal danger to his own view of the world and to the four main features of his (or, rather, Engels' and Lenin's) dialectic, according to which the universe had to be controlled, together with all the matter in it, including, most important of all, the uncomprehending human herd.

Conditions in that part of the world have, it is true, changed since Stalin. Today we would have to pry into every corner of Eastern and Western Europe before we could find a Marxist who would display such arbitrary, mountebank, crass stupidity in his attitude toward the theory of relativity and the picture of the world it projects. But in Stalin's time there were Marxists who devoted considerable intellectual effort, if nothing else, to using the theory of relativity and other scientific discoveries as a way of reinvigorating the aging Marxist formulas, which had been unable to incorporate satisfactorily even the scientific advances of the nineteenth century. But most of these men were branded as revisionists and silenced or put to death in concentration camps. Ironically, Lenin himself had in fact belonged to this group. In 1933, Sima Marković, one of the Yugoslav Communist leaders after World War I, was reminiscing to a group of young Communists. I was one of those young Communists with him, then fellow prisoners in the Ada Ciganlija Prison. Marković told us that when Lenin heard he was a mathematics professor Lenin suggested, during some Comintern congress, that he ought to tackle the problem of interpreting the theory of relativity from a Marxist standpoint. Marković did so. In spite of his Marxist frame of reference, he produced, under our backward Balkan conditions, what is perhaps the most distinguished popularization of Einstein's theory. He was a "rightist," however, and was later "liquidated" in the Soviet Union. In Yugoslavia today no one recognizes these facts.

This can indicate the difference between Lenin and Stalin in their approach to science. Lenin in the early days of the Communist state still had to fight in a hostile world, and in science, as in the real world, he sought to "discover" evidence to support his *a priori* truths. Stalin actually ruled one world, and because he was secure in his position he rejected or suppressed everything that did not conform to his own dogmas. The same difference occurred in their attitude to Marxist theoreticians: Lenin encouraged them and wrangled with them; Stalin transformed them into intellectual slaves or else liquidated them. But apart from this circumstance, extremely important from the political and social point of view in those times (and in our own times, too, unfortunately), there are no basic differences between the Leninist and the Stalinist methods, or between Lenin and Stalin themselves as regards their conviction that Marxism provides the means for making accurate forecasts of the world, of society, and of man.

It should not, therefore, come as a surprise that Stalin's presentation of Marxist philosophy—dialectical materialism—is the main target of my criticism. But this does not mean that I shall neglect the philosophical expositions of the other great Marxists, particularly Marx himself, and Engels and Lenin. It is a relatively simple task in that no great revolutionary Marxist before Stalin presented the whole of Marxist philosophy in a condensed form. Stalin was moved to undertake this not by any inner compulsion but from the sheer necessity of reconciling his absolute power with the absolutes of Marxist dogma. The view of the world he presented is important to my theme because he himself was an embodiment of the development of Communism from idea to actual power, and because no Marxist of major caliber has appeared since Stalin, or is likely to appear.

Here I should make clear that this book is not intended either as an exposition or as a refutation of Marxism. It is, rather, a disclosure of the inevitability of violence and corruption in human beings—in the mass and as individuals—once Marxism in its totality is applied to society, or, more strictly speaking, is imposed upon society. And since this chapter is devoted to a comparison of the Marxist view of the world with what can be called the relativity picture of the world, I must make it clear that, even were I a physicist and mathematician, which I am not, I would not seek to interpret the theory of relativity from some personal point of view of my own, except insofar as I need to explain certain quotations from scientific works for the sake of greater clarity.

Now I must plunge into the theme of this chapter.

As opposed to today's "saviors" and "restorers" of the "original" and "unalienated" Marxism, who have turned with all the malevolence of deluded fanatics thirsting for self-punishment against Stalin's "Dialectical and Historical Materialism," published in 1938 in *The History of the All-Union Communist Party (Bolsheviks)*, my researches lead me precisely to that work. In spite of his protosacerdotal and pragmatic simplifications, in this work Stalin sets out the unadulterated view on Marxist philosophical materialism and the Marxist dialectical method of his predecessors Engels and Lenin, and, in essence, Marx as well.

Stalin's treatment of Marxist materialism can be reduced to the theory that the world is: (a) material; (b) objectively real, *i.e.,* independent of human thought; (c) known. He establishes his method from these premises: (a) everything is determined and interconnected; (b) everything is in constant change; (c) the change takes place "as a forward and upward movement, as a transition from an old qualitative state to a new qualitative state, as a development from the simple to the complex, from the lower to the higher";[1] (d) everything is characterized by the struggle of opposites, which "constitutes the internal content of the transformation of quantitative changes into qualitative changes."[2]

Later critics accuse Stalin of having omitted one very important Engels-Lenin feature of the dialectic—the negation of the negation. This requires a brief explanation. The dialectic is a method of reasoning, *based on reality,* whereby opposites are brought into a new for-

1. *The History of the All-Union Communist Party (Bolsheviks),* Zagreb, 1945, p. 114.
2. *Ibid.,* p. 116.

mulation. Phenomena proceed from thesis to antithesis to synthesis. But every synthesis is said to generate its own contradiction and is thus "negated." For example, capitalism is the negation of feudalism, but at the same time socialism is the negation of capitalism, *i.e.*, the negation of the negation of feudalism. Thus this process becomes the "law" of the dialectic. The accusation that Stalin omitted this law is factually indisputable but it is also irrelevant, as is the fact that Lenin somewhere in his *Philosophical Notebooks* cites sixteen elements of the dialectic. What is in question is not the number of features in the dialectic, or the relative importance of any of them, but the dialectic itself, *i.e.*, the theory that nature, society, and man can be reduced to certain "regulations," "laws," and "attributes," all originating within the human brain.

As far as I am concerned, however, it is indisputable that Stalin did include, indirectly, the "negation of the negation" in his interpretation, so that his dialectical-materialist view of the world can be summed up as follows: the world objectively exists solely as a material world, and it can be comprehended; within this world everything is interdependent and in a constant progressive flux whereby through a struggle of opposites quantitative changes become transformed into qualitative changes.

But Marxism-Leninism did not stop at this not very imaginative picture of the world and everything that lives and thinks in it. As with all doctrines that have become instruments for the glorification and defense of entrenched social relationships, or social privileges, Marxism, too, has become increasingly constricted, vulgarized, and dogmatic. Compared with Stalin, Khrushchev is a vulgarizer, while Mao Tse-tung is an even more unquestioning dogmatist. For Khrushchev, as for all revisionists, the Marxist dialectic almost completely disappeared, which was why Soviet science was to some extent able to escape from Stalin's dialectical mold and concentration-camp methods. Mao Tse-tung, still committed to Marxism, has managed to "discover" the "basic law of the universe." Mao has declared that "Marxist philosophy maintains that the law of the unity of opposites is the basic law of the universe. This law has universal application, whether in the natural world, in human society, or in human thought."

Einstein's picture of the world is quite different and—happily for the human race—has nothing to say about any "basic law of the universe." Referring to Werner Heisenberg's law of indeterminacy, Einstein says that "as has been convincingly shown by Heisenberg, from an empirical point of view any conclusion about a strictly deterministic structure of the natural world is excluded once and for all. . . ." [3] Einstein proceeds to declare that "Classical physics introduced two substances: matter and energy. The first had weight, but the second was weightless. In classical physics we had two conservation laws: one for matter, the other for energy. . . . According to the theory of relativity, there is no essential distinction between mass and energy. Energy

3. In *Conceptions Scientifiques, Morales et Sociales*, Paris, 1962, p. 122.

has mass and mass represents energy." [4] Further: "Our physical space as conceived through objects and their motion has three dimensions, and positions are characterized by three numbers. The instant of an event is the fourth number. . . . The world of events forms a *fourth-dimensional continuum*. There is nothing mysterious about this, and the last sentence is equally true for classical physics and the relativity theory. Again a difference is revealed when two CS [Co-ordinate Systems] moving relatively to each other are considered. The room is moving, and the observers inside and outside determine the time-space co-ordinates of the same events. Again the classical physicist splits the four-dimensional continua into three-dimensional spaces and the one-dimensional time-continuum. The old physicist bothers only about the space transformation, as time is absolute for him. He finds the splitting of the four-dimensional world-continua into space and time natural and convenient. But from the point of view of the relativity theory, time as well as space is changed by passing from one CS to another." [5] Einstein posited these statements: "Every event that happens in the world is determined by the space-co-ordinates x, y, z, and the time-co-ordinate t. Thus the physical description was four-dimensional right from the beginning. . . . The four-dimensional continuum of space cannot be split up into a time-continuum and a space-continuum except in an arbitrary way. . . .

4. Albert Einstein and Leopold Infeld, *The Evolution of Physics*, New York, 1961, p. 197.

5. *Ibid.*, pp. 207–208.

Through the general theory of relativity, however, the view that the continuum is infinite in its time-like extent but finite in its space-like extent has gained in probability." [6] ". . . space and time are welded together into a uniform four-dimensional continuum." [7] "Matter has a granular structure; it is composed of elementary particles, the elementary quanta of matter. Thus, the electrical charge has a granular structure, and . . . so has energy. Photons are the energy quanta of which light is composed. Is light a wave or a shower of photons? These fundamental questions are forced upon physics by experiment. In seeking to answer them we have to abandon the description of atomic events as happening in space and time, we have to retreat still further from the old mechanical view. Quanta physics formulates laws governing crowds and not individuals. Not properties but probabilities are described, not laws disclosing the future of systems are formulated, but laws governing the changes in time of the probabilities and relating to great congregations of individuals." [8]

Quoting so extensively from Einstein, and indeed seeming to base much of my argument on his explanations, does not mean that I believe that Einstein's picture of the world is definitive or complete. I realize that contemporary physicists have gone beyond Einstein and, indeed, have called into question some of his postulates. Einstein and Einsteinian physics are used by me to char-

6. Albert Einstein, "Space-Time," Encyclopaedia Britannica.
7. Ibid.
8. Einstein and Infeld, op. cit., p. 297.

acterize and symbolize the achievements of modern science—achievements realized *at the same* time that Lenin and Stalin formulated their "laws of dialectics."

Accordingly, it is important to recognize at first glance the divergence between the picture of the world provided by Marxist philosophy and that given us by Einstein, or by modern science. Admittedly, they have certain features in common: objective reality and the possibility that the world can be gradually understood and changed. So while these features are not peculiar to Marxism, even less are they a Marxist discovery. They are the general postulates of every exact science; we find them formulated as far back as Aristotle and they were dogmatically entrenched in the French materialists of the eighteenth century. But what is peculiar to Marxism, what is its discovery—Hegel's dialectic "set on its feet," *i.e.,* made materialistic—finds little confirmatory evidence, except for a few findings in historical and sociological research.

The struggle of opposites in material objects and natural phenomena is encountered only as a product of human mental processes and experience, *i.e.,* as a human phenomenon and, therefore, a social phenomenon. It can also be said of the "forward and upward movement" (according to my earlier quotation of Stalin) that, as far as the natural world itself is concerned, "higher" and "lower" forms do not exist, that these are just assumptions about the natural world made on the basis of our human knowledge and conceptions of time—from the history of men, things, and phenomena, including the whole universe, whose forms have obviously been in a state of constant change in accordance with laws of which we are beginning to gain an increasingly profound understanding, since we are endowed with limitless powers of cognition; but we can never gain a final understanding because of the measureless dimensions and innumerable aspects of the real world, to which, of course, man himself belongs. Furthermore, feeling, thought, and consciousness, which Engels and Lenin called "the highest product of matter organized in a special way," [9] are the highest forms and products for us men according to our conceptions. If the natural world, *i.e.*, matter, could think, it would roar with laughter at human conceit, because it would know that our brains and senses are merely mass-energy differently arranged and brought into a set of relations different from that in any other inanimate or animate object, and are thus endowed with different potentialities. The conceptions men have of the universe and of the substances and phenomena inside it are always determined: they are the product of the sum total of men's knowledge, experiences, and imagination. But the universe and the phenomena and substances in it are what they are regardless of the picture of them that we build up and regardless of the inferences that we draw about them. . . .

I reached these conclusions in 1953, but until now I have had no opportunity to express them publicly. I did, just once, state my doubts, in such a way that I was challenged to express them, indeed by Tito himself. During my last meeting, in mid-January 1954, with the other three Secretaries of the Yugoslav Communist League,

9. V. I. Lenin, *Materialism and Empirio-criticism*, p. 47.

Tito, Kardelj, and Ranković, in connection with my "ideological deviations," which was to be followed shortly by my expulsion from the Central Committee and my dismissal from the office of President of the Federal Assembly, I happened to mention that modern science did not confirm the dialectic of the natural world. Tito made a brisk rejoinder, asking: "Are you willing to repeat that in public?" To which I replied that I was. And that is what I am doing now, even recognizing that Tito himself no longer believes in the dialectic, or, if he does, he no longer feels the necessity of defending it.

But if I was able to acquire this knowledge, all by myself, and at a time when I was in an isolated position in the Yugoslav Communist League, others had done so much earlier: Z. Richtman, in Yugoslavia, just before the war, for example, and Jean-Paul Sartre, in his *La critique de la raison dialectique.* Nevertheless, the similarity, even identity, between my own views of 1953 on the dialectic of the natural world and what I have recently read in Sartre moves me to deal with the present differences between him and me in our view of the dialectical method as a whole. Just as at that time I lacked the knowledge and the courage of my convictions, or did not yet feel the vital urge to shed the Hegelian-Marxist conception of the dialectical movement of society and human thought, in the same way Sartre remained at a halfway point (by rejecting the dialectic of the natural world and in many ways actually taking a step backward), and he created an artificial bridge between Marxism and his own version of existentialism, speculating in political terms about "enriching" Marxism with his own theories.

Sartre's rejection of the Engels dialectic of nature is so convincing, although expressed with the complexity of German philosophy, that it deserves to be studied. "The spirit sees the dialectic as the law of the world," he writes. "The result of that is that it again falls into complete dogmatic idealism. Indeed, scientific laws are experimental hypotheses verified by fact. As opposed to that, the absolute principle that the natural world is dialectical" cannot today be verified by any method. If you declare that a set of laws discovered by scientists constitutes a certain dialectical movement in the objects of those laws, Sartre says, you have no valid means at your disposal for proving it.[10] Neither laws nor "grand theories" will change, whatever way you may observe them. We, in fact, know, he continues, that the idea of the dialectic came into history by quite different paths, that Hegel and Marx discovered and defined it in terms of the relations between man and matter and of the reciprocal relationships between men. It was not until later, out of the desire for integration, that there was an attempt to discover the movement of human history in natural history. Thus, the assertion that the dialectic of

10. According to Sartre, all these observations obviously refer only to the dialectic taken as an abstract and universal law of nature. When it comes to human history, to the contrary, the dialectic retains its heuristic value. It is latent, maintaining its control by establishing the facts, and it reveals itself by integrating them and enabling them to be comprehended; this comprehension discloses a new dimension of history, and finally its truth and intelligibility.

the natural world exists will depend on the sum total of material facts—past, present, and future, or, if you wish, it is followed by the integration of temporality.[11]

Sartre examines the dialectic in this way: "But let us examine what Engels tells us about 'the most general laws of natural history and social history.' He says:

'We can reduce them to three basic laws:
The law of the passing of quantity into quality, and vice-versa;
The law of the reciprocal interpenetration of opposites;
The law of the negation of the negation.'

All these three laws were developed by Hegel in his idealistic way as simple laws of thought. . . . The error lies in trying to impose these laws on the natural world and history as laws of thought, instead of extracting laws from them.

"Engels' uncertainty can be seen in the words he used: to abstract does not mean to deduce. And how could universal laws be deduced from a collection of particular laws? This, if you like, is called induction. We have seen that in nature we find in fact only the dialectic that we have placed there. . . . Engels accuses Hegel of imposing the laws of thought on matter; and his reason for that is that he himself is compelling the sciences to confirm the dialectical reason which he had discovered in the world of society. Yet, in the world of history and society, as we shall see, the dialectical reason is indeed at

11. There is an internal integration of temporality seen as the sum and substance of history, but that is something quite different, says Sartre.

issue; by bringing it into the 'natural' world, forcibly stamping it there, Engels removes its rationality; it is no longer a question of the dialectic which man created in creating himself, and which for its part creates him, but of a chance law of which all that can be said is: 'That is how it is, not otherwise.' " [12]

In the history of human thought it would be difficult to find anything more nonsensical than the Marxist doctrine on the dialectic of nature; yet, for all that, it has, by supplementing Marxist ideology, played a tremendous role in social struggles. This could well lead one to take a rather dim view of human beings and their intelligence. But we can take comfort in the knowledge that for people, that is to say human communities, what appear to them to be the greatest truths and most majestic thoughts are the beliefs and symbols that carry them to salvation and victory.

The situation is not the same, though it is similar, with Marxist philosophical materialism, which continues to resist the teeth of time and the fury of heretical critics. This is so mainly because no one contests its basic postulates—the substantiality and objectivity of the natural world, the dependence of thought upon the brain and the sensory organs—which were taken over from the French materialists and Ludwig Feuerbach, and then demechanized by making a bridge with the Hegelian dialectic. In fact, the only disputable point here is the Marxist conception of matter, which is defined, as we have seen, on the one hand as a dialectical reality and on

12. "The Dogmatic Dialectic and the Critical Dialectic," *Delo*, Belgrade, June 6, 1966, Vol. XII, pp. 794–799.

the other as an objective reality presented sensuously exclusively. Thus, we find Lenin, following Engels, giving this definition in *Materialism and Empirio-criticism:* "The concept of matter is exclusively the expression of objective reality given to our senses," and saying further: "Matter is a philosophical category for denoting the objective reality presented to man in his sensations, which our senses copy, photograph and reflect, and which exist independently of them."

It is this attachment to matter of the dialectical label, printed in the usual way as being exclusive and irrevocable truth, that makes this view unscientific and dogmatic in itself. But even the conception of matter as an "objective reality presented to man in his sensations," *i.e.,* through his senses, "which our senses copy, photograph and reflect," is, by its very simplification, to some degree unscientific and dogmatic.

The philosophical concept of matter could, for Lenin as for all good Marxists, be reduced to an objectivity which, while independent of the senses, is perceived by them. It should be added that this conception was not new; as soon as Engels and Lenin forget about the dialectic, or cease their materialistic idolization of it, they speak the language of the nineteenth century. Furthermore, all Marxists know, and no one else denies it, that the Marxist view of the world, and consequently of matter, is a marriage of eighteenth-century materialism and the Hegelian idealist dialectic. Lenin actually stresses this in his "Three Sources and Three Component Parts of Marxism": "But Marx did not stop at eighteenth-century materialism; he pushed philosophy forward. He enriched it with the achievements of German classical philosophy, particularly the Hegelian system. . . . The greatest of these achievements is the dialectic."

On consideration today, this materialism "enriched" by Hegel's idealist dialectic seems rather grotesque to me. Particularly revealing is the recognition that the doctrine manifestly did not arise out of new thinking about matter. It arose from other motivations, not scientific or philosophical ones, but, rather, social and political ones: new social forces and upheavals in society imposed the need for the construction of a new ideology, which, like other social doctrines, could only be shaped from appropriate notions already extant. This may lessen Marx's stature as an original philosopher, but it makes him all the greater as a revolutionary and social thinker. . . .

Quite obviously, therefore, such an ideological conception, the conception of determined social groups, cannot be maintained, because, first, it loses its core—the "holy spirit" of matter, i.e., the dialectic, in accord with historical changes and the determined needs of society—and, second, its "sensory-perceptive" side imposes changes according to new scientific knowledge about the "divinity" itself, matter.

In making this criticism, however, I have no intention of rejecting the physical nature of the world, and certainly not its objectivity. Something else, something new and more important, is at issue: modern physics has brought the concept of matter into reciprocal relation with energy, thus dispensing with the static conceptions of it that Engels and Lenin had evidently retained in spite of all their shrewdness and in spite of the dialectical approach adopted by them. Until the eighteenth century, and even later, it was possible to define matter. But since that time many definitions have evaporated. Today it would be difficult to contrive a definition that would embrace all the kaleidoscopic and objective insubstantiality of matter. Neither Einstein nor any other great scientist, unlike Engels and Lenin, has been bold enough to undertake such a task as a definitive definition, their reluctance being all the greater because such an attempt would have hindered, rather than helped, their work and their role in society. Since I have never felt kinship with any eternal spirit, and have rejected God-created matter, I do not deny objective reality and a mental perception of the world; but I cannot accept a mystical dialectic or the rational mechanistic interpretation. Matter does not "vanish," as was thought by the empirio-critics, or, rather, the Russian Machists,[13] who were criticized by Lenin; knowledge about it has been amended and supplemented: "pure matter," matter that is not energy, does not exist in our conceptions, and energy itself is shown to be material. Even if the

13. A term coined from the surname of Ernst Mach, Austrian physicist and philosopher, whose criticism of the Newtonian legacy paved the way for Einstein's relativity theory, and was one of the sources of the logical positivism of the so-called Vienna Circle. Ernst Mach and the Russian Machists were severely criticized, in *Materialism and Empirio-criticism,* by Lenin, who took the position of the dogmatic dialectical materialism of Engels; so that "Machism" is represented today by Soviet ideologists as the essence and symbol of "idealist," *i.e.,* hostile, intellectual poison, though they are ignorant of its postulates.

very complex instruments, including computers, which have been giving us a whole range of new insights into the nature of matter are regarded as extensions of our sensory organs and our organ of thought, the brain, we still cannot reduce the concept of matter to the data, images, and inferences that we obtain from matter as such.

No boundaries can be set to human thought. Human thinking inquires into the nature of matter, sometimes successfully and accurately, taking the data received through the sensory organs, or by means of instruments, as the essential facts from which inferences can be drawn, theories elaborated, and scientific laws laid down. Einstein arrived at his relativity theory without instruments, laboratories, or experiments—with just a pencil and paper and the power of his thought, aided, of course, by knowledge he had acquired from others. (And Newton worked in an analogous way, because he was obviously not in a position to measure gravitation by means of the senses.) Einstein did not arrive at his relativity theory by experiment but through thought; and many, I am right in adding, consider his discovery to be as much a philosophical as a scientific theory. In the history of modern thought the same dual role has been played by the Copernican system, Newton's law of gravitation, Darwin's researches into the origin of species, and Marx's researches into the economic basis of society.

Finally, I will mention this: every modern psychologist knows that the perception of matter is not the simple "photography" of Lenin's system. Matter is certainly independent of what people, including Lenin, think about it; but we *know* nothing about it except what we have arrived at through science and meditations. Contemporary human knowledge is not only at variance with the Engels-Lenin thesis; it actually refutes it. Thus, the definition of matter, like knowledge about it, is subject to change and can never be reduced to a product of sense perception. Knowledge about matter is one aspect of man's total knowledge of the world and is different in every age and in every great thinker. Bertrand Russell has come to this conclusion in his *History of Western Philosophy:*

"What is important to the philosopher in the theory of relativity is the substitution of space-time for space and time. Common sense thinks of the physical world as composed of 'things' which persist through a certain period of time and move in space. Philosophy and physics developed the notion of 'thing' into that of 'material substance,' and thought of material substance as consisting of particles, each very small, and each persisting throughout all time. Einstein substituted events for particles; each event had to each other a relation called 'interval,' which could be analysed in various ways into a time-element and a space-element. The choice between these various ways was arbitrary, and no one of them was theoretically preferable to any other. Given two events A and B, in different regions, it might happen that according to one convention they were simultaneous, according to another A was earlier than B, and according to yet another B was earlier than A. No physical facts correspond to these different conventions.

"From all this it seems to follow that events, not particles, must be the 'stuff' of physics. What has been thought of as a particle will have to be thought of as a series of events. The series of events that replaces a particle has certain important physical properties, and therefore demands our attention; but it has no more substantiality than any other series of events that we might arbitrarily single out. Thus 'matter' is not part of the ultimate material of the world, but merely a convenient way of collecting events into bundles. . . .

"While physics has been making matter less material, psychology has been making mind less mental. We had occasion in a former chapter to compare the association of ideas with the conditioned reflex. The latter, which has replaced the former, is obviously much more physiological. (This is only one illustration; I do not wish to exaggerate the scope of the conditioned reflex.) Thus from both ends physics and psychology have been approaching each other, and making more possible the doctrine of 'neutral monism' suggested by William James's criticism of 'consciousness.' The distinction of mind and matter came into philosophy from religion, although, for a long time, it seemed to have valid grounds. I think that both mind and matter are merely convenient ways of grouping events. Some single events, I should admit, belong only to material groups, but others belong to both kinds of groups, and are therefore at once mental and material. This doctrine effects a great simplification in our picture of the structure of the world." [14]

The inadequacy and unscientific character of the Engels-Lenin formula of "copying, photographing, and reflecting" objective reality becomes most notorious

14. New York, 1959, pp. 832–833.

when applied to reality and to human thought itself. How have men been able to change history if they are inseparable from what they are "copying"? Was not Lenin himself inspired by his vision of a new world to change "objective reality"? And did Lenin really believe that Plato amounted to nothing because of his view that knowledge could not be gained through the senses but had to be sought by the mind? And can a work of art be reduced to a matter of "copying, photographing, and reflecting" objective reality? Would it in any sense be *art* if it kept within Lenin's definition of matter and matter's "reflecting" properties? Every turnip has a root; Lenin's theory of reflection is the basis for so-called "socialist realism," and the dogmatic stupefication of whole generations and the violation of the human mind are thus "convincingly" justified by Engels and Lenin. . . .

In spite of this, we human beings have cause to be proud of what we know about nature, even when we attribute our own laws to it and try to force it to fit our own schemata. Although Hegelian-Marxist dialectics and mechanistic-Marxist materialism have not advanced the human intellect one single inch in its exploration of nature, they have, by being the heart and soul of revolutionary ideology, played an epoch-making role in changing contemporary human society and, inevitably, international relations. But in all this, dialectics and materialism have been symbols of faith, not philosophical or scientific truths.

Not only is it not essential for religions and creeds, even in the periods of their ascendancy, to be in tune with scientific truths, it is not even crucial for them if they are actually in open conflict with science: Christianity triumphed, although it was not in tune with the philosophies and science of the ancient world. The same thought holds good when an ideology or religion proves its truth by recourse to science, *i.e.*, pseudo science, and believes in its own scientism. Hitler's racialism strengthened its positions by recourse to "scientific proofs" and theories; and Topitsch has produced convincing evidence that, "by attaching itself to Hegel's ideas, an expressly authoritarian, anti-liberal and anti-democratic doctrine of power developed in Germany, stretching in an unbroken tradition throughout the last century, gaining considerable influence in the Kaiser Wilhelm era, and finally, in the preparations for Hitler's regime and service to it, playing a role that should not be minimized." [15]

Although ideology and science are inevitable and inseparable aspects of man's way of life, they differ in respect of their subject matter. Ideology is concerned with man's struggle against man, and science with his struggle against nature. They differ also in their aspirations and methods, for ideology is predominantly irrational and ideal, while science is rational and real. By appearing at a time of revolutionary scientific discoveries, which altered man's environment as well as his outlook on nature, Marxism could only be made meaningful as an ideology, and acceptable as a "science" or philosophy, if it were "based on scientific achievements," the more so because

15. Ernst Topitsch, *Die Sozialphilosophie Hegels als Heislehre- und Herrschaftsideologie,* Berlin, 1967, p. 63, quoted in *Knjizevne Novine,* Belgrade, April 13, 1968, Vol. XX, No. 325, p. 9.

its creator, Marx, was both a revolutionary and the founder of social science. Other doctrines, including socialist, religious, and utopian ones, had failed to show the proletarianized strata of society—as well as the minor, dependent nations—a way out of their poverty and despair. There was a favorable opportunity for the Marxist doctrine more or less to arrogate to itself the role of a new faith, and a scientific one at that. Heraclitus observed that nature likes to remain hidden; and, we could add, particularly as regards human purposes and actions. From historical perspectives and conditions of human existence, Marxist philosophy presents itself as a rationalistic, scientized mystique.

V

There is one question in urgent need of an answer:
Why has no one in the Communist movement even attempted to close the yawning gap between the picture of
the world presented by modern physics and the one so
recklessly imposed by Communist leaders and dogmatists? This question is unavoidable because a similar conflict exists between the other exact sciences and Marxist-
Leninist doctrines, and in a later chapter I will show
that the same situation applies between the social sciences and Marxism-Leninism. The most notorious example of this is the resistance put up by Stalin's protégé
Trofim D. Lysenko to modern genetics, although other,
less artless and harmless, sciences have fared no better in
the Procrustean bed of the dialectical bosses. It is important to note that this bludgeoning and mutilation of
scientific research is the obverse of the much fiercer vic-
timization of modern art, which some bureaucratic Communist potentates, usually arrogating to themselves the
role of high priests, deride and suppress.

In its early days, Marxism was not in such drastic conflict with scientific views on the structure and mutation of the world, society, and man. After the Kant-Laplace theory of the evolutionary beginnings of the solar system and the earth, the Lamarck-Darwin discoveries of the continuous transformation of living species, the demonstrations by the French materialists of the primacy and objectivity of matter, the teachings of Comte and others on progress in society, Hegel's interpretation of history as a struggle of opposites, Mignet's generalization of the French Revolution as a class war, and, lastly but not the least important, the unmistakable formation of the proletariat into a separate class—after all this, it seemed incontrovertible that everything moved, and moved upward, and it was even possible to make a convincing defense of the theory that not only is the world objective but also it exists precisely as we perceive it through our sensory organs, and that the struggle of opposites is the spirit of movement inside it. The intellectual climate of the eighteenth century and even of a considerable part of the nineteenth consisted of belief in reason, progress, and freedom. Similar socialist theories—like those of Fourier, Owen, Proudhon—emerged to satisfy the vital needs of the new proletarian social forces and the new socialist political movements; but I only mention these in passing, although they were most decisive for the establishment and success of the dialectical-materialist point of view.

Once established as a complete and universal theory, or, to be accurate, as an ideology, Marxism failed to be *current.* In spite of its obsession with dialectics and materialism, Marxism failed to keep abreast of new discoveries even to the extent that it had done in its early days. It failed, indeed, to make the critical appraisals characteristic of Marx himself.

Moreover, Marx had not formulated his theories as a philosophy, as a finished, closed ideational system. Each of his works deals with a particular area or theme, or is an analysis of contemporary historical events. Not a single purely philosophical piece of writing by him exists that has any bearing on the exact sciences. His philosophical writing was always parenthetical and, strictly, was influenced by some discovery relating to social conditions or social theories. Although it cannot be said that Marx's friend Engels and Marx's followers distorted the essence of his views, it is no accident that he himself failed to systematize them. Marx was sufficiently learned and wise not to divorce himself in his researches from concrete historical reality and his own social science; he sought confirmation for his general theories primarily there. His picture of the real world and the sciences suffered somewhat because of this, but at least they were not transformed into abstract "ultimate" truths.

Marxism is, in a sense, the only "complete" dogma of modern times. There is as yet no explanation—and never will be an exact one—for the unexpected emergence, after medieval Scholasticism, of a dogmatized conception of the world and the human spirit. Yet within Marxism itself the number and nature of the conflicts between various Marxist systematizers and science, and how these conflicts arose, can be reliably established.

But I shall confine myself to the bare essentials in examining this problem and following my thoughts.

The first systematization of Marxism was undertaken by Marx's closest collaborator, Friedrich Engels, in *Anti-Dühring*, a work that Marx read very closely and approved of, and which, as Engels himself admits, was written for the express purpose of serving practical party needs. He states unequivocally in his book *Anti-Dühring:* "Three years ago, when Dühring, an adherent, and once a reformer, of socialism, suddenly threw down a challenge to his century, my friends in Germany kept entreating me to write a critical examination of this new socialist theory for *Volksstaat,* at that time the central organ of the Social Democratic party. They considered this of overriding importance in order to prevent the party, which was still young and only recently united, from again falling into sectarian schism and disorder."

That was how the codifier of "Communist ideology" —he was also, by the way, the inventor of the actual term—confirmed the conclusion reached by reasoning on the nature of Communism, and every other ideology that followed it—namely, Communist ideology did not arise out of scientific motives but from definite political, party needs. It was only subsequently dressed up and presented as a science, as a scientific view of the world. Thus, with Engels' *Anti-Dühring* was born a dogma, necessary to the socialist movement and party; thus began the silencing of every consistent, impartial scientific scholarship in it. . . . And to complete the picture of this "science," it must be added that not one single major Marxist theoretician or interpreter of the science has been a scientist; and every Marxist who has taken up his pen to expound his "science," or to apply it to other sciences, has done so, more often than not, as a routine party duty, but never because he was inspired as a theoretician. From the time of Engels to the present day every impartial investigation, even on a quasi-scientific basis, has been proscribed; everything is subordinated to the current practical needs of the party, or, rather, of the party faction in power. In view of this state of affairs, it is not difficult for people of limited knowledge (like Todor Zhivkov, in Bulgaria, and Wladyslaw Gomulka, in Poland) to become watchdogs of theoretical purity. This inevitably leads to the vulgarization of the original Marxism, and to the disappointment and defection of the best brains in the movement. The dogma has become part of the power structure, with the leader, by right, its high priest, like a caliph or sultan in Islam. Not even Engels, for all his wide scope and multifarious culture, was, at the time of writing *Anti-Dühring* (1877) and sketching out *The Dialectics of Nature* (in the 1870's), completely in the stream of important discoveries in physics and the other sciences, let alone in a position to interpret them accurately.

With the development of the socialist movement after Engels, a whole host of theoreticians appeared in various countries: Karl Johann Kautsky, Rosa Luxemburg, and Franz Mehring in Germany, Paul Lafargue and Jean Jaurès in France, G. V. Plekhanov in Russia, Antonio Labriola in Italy, Viktor Adler in Austria, Dimitr Blagoev in Bulgaria, and others. Some of them were talented leaders, ingenious polemicists, informed interpreters in various fields of study, but not one of these could make a vital contribution to actual theory. The only exceptions to have been partially justified by history are Eduard Bernstein, in the West, who analyzed the possibilities for the reform and peaceful transformation of capitalism, and Lenin, in the East, with his theory of the revolutionary party and his practice of revolution. It is worthwhile, here, to repeat that socialist theory in Britain developed mainly through the non-Marxist Fabian Society, while in the United States there has not been, for practical purposes, any socialist movement at all; and this in spite of the fact that these two countries have the highest-developed working class—a proof that Marxism is not a socialist theory of universal validity, and that, contrary to Marxist assumptions, the working class is not bound to adopt socialist ideas.

Although even the revisionists of the revolutionary, dialectical side of Marxian doctrine have had no more success in their expositions of the real problems of the world, what interests us here are those who have remained faithful, *i.e.*, the dogmatic Communists, since their opinions and organized power still represent a presence in social and international relations.

The most important of these are Lenin, Stalin, and Mao Tse-tung.

When in 1908 Lenin published *Materialism and Empirio-criticism,* his only important work that can claim to be philosophical, the theory of relativity, which had been published in 1905, was hardly known, except to a narrow circle of experts, who, more often than not, regarded it as a controversial theory. So Lenin can hardly be blamed for not having included it in his studies. But he was intellectually active right up to 1922 (he died in

1924), and in his numerous works—all teeming with dialectical and materialist observations—no examination of the quantum theory or the relativity theory is anywhere to be found, the names of Planck and Bohr are not even mentioned, and Einstein gets a bare two lines, parenthetically, as it were—for this was at a time he was attacking "fashionable" European philosophers who had "taken up Einstein." In *Materialism and Empiriocriticism,* and in later philosophical allusions, he defends Marx's philosophical views, and Engels' even more, without in any way modifying their essentials, and, more significant, he does so by retaining from classical physics the Newtonian concept of the immutability of time and space, the three-dimensional nature of space, and so on. He was very perspicacious, and he realized that the theoretical researches and discoveries of modern physics were not in tune with his dialectical blueprints, which is the main reason he so often spoke of the "crisis in modern physics." How far his claims and predictions have proved accurate can be judged by the declaration of the great physicist J. Robert Oppenheimer that since the end of the last war science has made more important discoveries than in the whole of previous human history. It cannot be wondered that our concepts of the world and of human existence are changing! But in fact the crisis in the dialectical scheme of things was there, present and obvious, all the time, and Lenin was unable or unwilling to see it, because it would have imperiled the visions that were his breath of life and the guarantee of his genius. With admirable fervor and conviction he exposed, by means of quotations from Marx and Engels, the incongruities in the views of various doubters and skeptics; and indeed he was successful in this, though the philosophical picture of the world, even the Marxist one, was not enlarged or clarified as a result. He often derided the "philosophizing physicists," though his own role as a "physicizing philosopher" was much less enviable. Justice, however, must be done to Lenin: he was not a physicist; he had no specialist advisers; and he was so burdened with other tasks that he never succeeded in gaining a close acquaintance with the subject. But his successors have had time and they have had access to experts in abundance. Yet, in essence, they have only repeated what Engels and Lenin said, and they still go on doing it, deafening even their own ears with their histrionic protestations about how Lenin with his genius had generalized the achievements of modern science.

Of Stalin's philosophical generalizations enough has already been said. As for Mao Tse-tung's views, as far as I have been able to see, they are original only on matters of guerrilla warfare, while in everything else they bear the stigma of being an even greater oversimplification, albeit expressed with a force of conviction that can be compared only with Lenin's.

Thus, the philosophical foundations of Marxism, laid down in the mid-nineteenth century and systemized by the eighteen-seventies, have remained in essence unchanged, while the modern sciences have been pushing forward inexorably. Engels' hope has not come to pass: "Materialism must change its form with every epochal discovery in the field of the natural sciences." And it could not have come to pass. Even if Marxism had not been transformed into the theory of the struggle for power, and then still later into the dogma of power, Marxist materialism is too firmly anchored to its Hegelian dialectical bedrock to be flexible enough to be brought into harmony with the sciences.

If this has proved impossible, have there not been skeptics and scientific experts within the Marxist movement who would proclaim this impossibility? There have been, to be sure, but these men either deluded themselves or were silenced—belief is stronger than fact, the needs of life more decisive than truth. Then, have there not been non-Marxist scientists in Communist countries who would point out the anomalous position? The scientists have indeed been aware of all this, but they have kept to the sidelines, or, more usually, have made declarations substantiating the authenticity of the dogma and the omniscience of the party leader, in the hope of escaping persecution and surviving in intellectual fields more durable and creditable than politics. After all, scientists are also human beings; they have to earn their living in a given social environment as it is, and although, like politicians, they talk too much about their consciences, in the final analysis they do what they can according to their principles. Over the years a convention has been worked out by which the scientists ostensibly confirm the congruity of their theories with Marxist-Leninist dogmas: in their public utterances they deliver eulogies to the "men of genius" who are their leaders and to the "wise men in leading positions," and their writings are sprinkled with quotations from the Marxist-Leninist "classics," *i.e.,* Marx, Engels,

Lenin, Stalin, Mao Tse-tung, and, of course, with mention of the current national leader in their own country —all this in order that their serious scientific analyses and the results of their research will get an entrance ticket to the public forum and to the universities.

But it must seem rather extraordinary that Marxist doctrine—in spite of the evidently ever-increasing anomalies between its basic postulates and the exact sciences—has managed to keep alive, and, in particular, has managed to strengthen the movement it inspires. As with other such instances in history, an exhaustive explanation of this "absurdity" cannot be given, for the simple reason that analyses of social phenomena inevitably carry with them, however scientific they may be, the views of those who made them; moreover, the continued existence of nations and of the human race involves the continual emergence of new facts and new knowledge. It seems to me that what has been at work here are matters of life and death for classes and nations which, owing to the "injustices of history," have fallen into hopeless poverty and decline. Prophets and prophesies are the progeny of despair. What matters to people leased out to slavery and slow death is not whether a certain picture of the world is true from the rational and scientific point of view, but whether it inspires them, whether it offers them any prospects of a change in their living conditions. It is more expedient, therefore, for a nation in increasing peril and for people who are increasingly disenfranchised to remain loyal to a teaching that has offered prospects of improvement, rather than to subject that teaching to scientific researches and comparisons.

The very idea of such a thing, of subjecting established theory to critical scrutiny, has been represented as treasonable—a charge that becomes incontestable for the believers, since those fighting for their vision of a better life are provided with convincing explanations in the field of social relations by Marxist theory, namely, the crises and conflicts into which state and social organisms have been drawn, in Russia and Yugoslavia, for instance. The essential here is belief, not exact truth. . . . This is reminiscent of Hegel's answer, when told that some parts of his system might not fit the facts: "So much the worse for the facts!" I can remember how my colleagues and I, as Communist leaders, whenever we heard any doubts about Marxist postulates, "knew" in advance that "revisionism," "the enemy," was at work. More important, the same holds good for Marxism in practice: there is no need for practice to be consistent with prevailing theory as long as it leads ineluctably to its objective. Herein lies the diabolical genius of Stalin: he realized that Communists, in spite of their troubled human consciences, would go along with his falsehoods and crimes because these were accepted as expedients and sacrifices that had to be made on the Communist party's journey to its true end. My doubts were first brought home to me when the Trotskyist trials opened in Moscow in 1936. But I convinced myself of the truth of the charges; otherwise I would not have remained in the movement to which I had dedicated myself, and which had made me its partisan through struggle, tribulation, and confinement in jail. When I suspected from Tito's reticence after his return from Moscow in 1938 that things were not quite as they had been represented there, I suppressed my moral doubts—that was how things ought to be, so that was how they must be. In the forefront of facts marched the *a priori* truths; and the struggle for their realization—indeed, for my own realization of myself—stifled the ethical sense and even became transformed into its own ethic, the highest ethic of all.

Communism is not a religion; and comparison between Communism and religion is inappropriate. But in the "absurdities" of Communism's rise to strength, there is something analogous with the situation of the Roman slaves and the colonial peoples of the Roman Empire. They were susceptible to a mystical belief in a Redeemer Son of God and his resurrection, whereas the Roman patricians, with their education in rationalistic and scientific Stoicism, could only ridicule it all as simplemindedness. The observation might be made that Christianity, unlike the modern ideologies, gave men the idea of equality and love, the idea of the identity of men's fates. This is true. But if in the past Christianity was able at times to predominate over the forces of hate and violence, in our time it has not been sufficient to stem the ideas of hatred and brute force. In our own times did not the irrational, sinister forces of Nazism sweep one of the most civilized nations in the world back to brutishness and infamy, bringing ruin upon Europe and a considerable part of the human race? And even today, in a different guise and with different motivations, are not the demons of violence and lawlessness, slavery and death, running riot?

Time, environment, and social needs have done their work: the incongruities between dialectics and science have made the Communists increasingly dogmatic as they struggle for power and a monopoly of power. Yet at the same time they have gained a greater sense of realism. The most creative founders of Communism were also the greatest, the most convinced, and the most "scientific" of the dogmatists. Thus, Lenin was more dogmatic than Engels; but he had a deeper, more nearly infallible feeling for the realities of his time, and for the revolutionary conditions in his own country, Russia. The same can be said about Stalin. The most dogmatic of them all is Mao Tse-tung; but he may well be the most realistic, because of his insight into China's destiny and his discernment of the way the dogma has degenerated in the hands of its carriers, owing to the human tendency to opt for what is easy and convenient. This self-destructive realism of Communists seems to become more powerful and infallible as its executives become more wedded to the dogma. While instilling a power of resistance to realities with its absoluteness, the dogma at the same time seeks an accommodation with realities in order to survive and conquer. This is how it is: the Communists are relentless, implacable dogmatists who boldly, deliberately, and doggedly appraise human situations and the opportunities there, and work on them with a ruthlessness that is turned even against themselves, as though they were all objects to be sacrificed to the predetermined objectives of history and human existence. So it can be said that the great founders of the dogma, the leading architects of Communism—Engels, Lenin, Stalin, and Mao Tse-tung—were not really dogmatists in the literal sense of the word. They are dogmatists only if considered from the changed conditions of today. For as long as men submit—as long as life does—to the dogma, it will continue to represent itself as a revelation, as a science. Until a dogma has the capacity to sanctify first its struggle, then its powers and privileges, it is not a dogma as far as its adherents are concerned. The turning point for Marxism came when modern technology and economic and political circumstances forced the Communists and their systems to come out of their shells, intellectually and practically, and, in a fight for survival, to become, themselves, "unbelievers" and "revisionists."

This is what has also happened with other revolutionary movements in the course of history. The only difference with the fortunes of Communism is that it came to the fore in the name of science and in the belief that it was a science—but that was because of its time, because of the structure imposed upon it by prevailing conditions, and because of the illusions with which it had to identify itself before it could become a reality.

VI

The disfigured and unreal face of dialectical materialism was first reflected in the mirror of the natural sciences, primarily theoretical physics. But these sciences
were powerless, by themselves, to present that face in its
true image until the right moment arrived, with the
suitable social conditions—until, in fact, the Communists themselves found it useful, indeed inevitable, to
recognize the results and proofs of scientific research.
Thus, the Soviet Union at the end of Stalin's rule had
reached the absurd position of producing nuclear bombs
while rejecting the implications of Einstein's theory of
relativity, which contains what has been called the
"basic equation for nuclear energy" and which is simply
one aspect of reality. Soviet students could not help
learning Einsteinian physics, because today there is no
alternative; and Soviet scientists, who are among the
most inventive and profound in the world, could only
blush for shame in front of their Western colleagues because of the imbecilities of official philosophical propaganda. Indeed, when things decay, they decay very nas-

tily. When China continues to justify itself and explain everything in the world according to the Maoist version of Marxism, attributing its success in producing both watermelons and nuclear bombs to the "omnipotent" and "omniscient" teachings of Mao Tse-tung, it is because of the ambitions of its revolutionary and despotic rulers to fight, tooth and nail, even with grotesque propaganda weapons, for their chosen way of life and the status of their country as a world power.

It is instructive for everyone, including the Chinese themselves, to understand how the change in attitude toward Einstein and his theory came about in the Soviet Union. But to avoid any misunderstandings, I must first of all point out that the relativity theory met with less resistance from scientists in the Soviet Union than in other countries, and that it was only the official ideologists and those scientists subordinated to them who opposed the theory's philosophical implications—the view of the world that it revealed—which are inseparable from its scientific inferences. The hard-core opposition lasted until Stalin's death, and it continues in a somewhat milder form even today, although this is a situation that has brought the Soviet ideologists into a ludicrous position.

Comparisons of the treatment of this problem under Stalin and Khrushchev in the most reputable Soviet scientific publications give a picture of what has changed—as well as what is still the same—in the rigid, imitative view of Soviet Marxists:

On Einstein, in 1933: "Einstein's philosophical position is not distinguished by consistency. Materialistic and dialectical views are intermixed with the Machist postulates that prevail in nearly all of E[instein]'s philosophical utterances. . . . He takes up the position of liberal democratism. He does not hide his sympathies for the USSR and is a member of the Soviet Friendship Association." [1]

On Einstein, in 1957: "Einstein's philosophical views are never presented in any sort of consistent form. His works retain their deep progressive significance regardless of this or that utterance of a philosophical nature." [2]

Thus, while Einstein's "philosophical views" and "positions" are openly attacked in 1933 as being Machist, in 1957 it is only alleged that he had never stated his views in a consistent form. The attitude toward Einstein's thoughts about the world on the basis of the relativity theory and other scientific learning has become milder and more tolerant, although there still remains a deep-rooted mistrust of his philosophical views, these being considered "unclear." As far as Soviet ideology is concerned, Einstein as a thinker has not risen above the level of a naïve liberal, a person suitable enough, perhaps, to become a member of the Soviet Friendship Association.

On the theory of relativity, in 1932: "A profound criticism of these views [Newton's views on time and space] was made by Engels, when he laid bare Newton's metaphysical outlook. In his analysis of the concept of mo-

1. Bolshaya Sovetskaya Enciklopedia, first ed., Moscow, Vol. 33, p. 154.
2. Bolshaya Sovetskaya Enciklopedia, second ed., Moscow, Vol. 48, p. 343.

tion, Engels points out: 'The motion of an isolated body does not exist; only relative motion exists.' (Marx and Engels: Works, vol. XIV, p. 393.) Because every motion, mechanical motion in particular, is the interaction of bodies. The concept of an absolute divorced from matter in motion in space and time is the same sort of metaphysical abstraction. Space and time are forms of the existence of matter in motion and have no existence as separate entities independent of matter. In this connection, Engels writes: 'Obviously both forms of the existence of matter [*i.e.*, space and time] are nothing more, without the matter itself, than empty concepts, an abstraction that exists only in our heads. . . .' This theory [the theory of relativity] is a step forward in the development of physics. —But it should be stressed here that the collapse of the old concepts of space and time, being linked up with the t.r., has been exploited by reactionary bourgeois philosophy, in particular Machism, and similar viewpoints tending towards subjective idealism. To a certain extent, help has been forthcoming for this from certain physicists, in particular the founder of the theory of relativity himself, Einstein. —Thus, Einstein has on several occasions presented his researches as a development of E. Mach's ideas on time and space. . . . Further, there is no foundation for the belief that the analysis of space-time made by Einstein is definitive and exhaustive. What is needed is a critical materialistic analysis of the t.r. and an inquiry into the literature of the t.r.'s existing postulates.'' [3]

3. Bolshaya Sovetskaya Enciklopedia, first ed., Moscow, Vol. 33, pp. 616–617.

On the theory of relativity, in 1955: "The theory of relativity is a physical theory of space and time, and closely connected with it are such basic physical concepts as motion, mass, energy etc.; thus, its general inferences have philosophical implications, and it cannot be understood without the necessary philosophical analysis of its foundations. Space and time are forms of the existence of matter; and that means that space relations and time relations have no intrinsic existence by themselves but are determined by material connections with objects and phenomena. Accordingly, the general laws of these relations, and of the properties of space and time, constitute the laws and properties of the general structure of the material connections of objects and phenomena. Accordingly, development of knowledge about the properties of space and time depends upon knowledge about the properties of matter itself. While the theory of space and time in classical physics derived mainly from knowledge of the properties and relations of solid bodies, the t.r. has grown up on the soil of research into electromagnetic processes. . . . Thus, at the basis of the t.r. lie new principles concerning the general properties of material connections, the interaction of physical phenomena. This means that the birth and development of the theory of relativity have served to confirm the doctrine of dialectical materialism on space and time as forms of the existence of matter. . . . —Dialectical materialism teaches that space and time are forms of the existence of matter. 'Nothing exists in the universe except matter in motion, and matter cannot move except in space and time' (Works of V. I. Lenin, fourth ed., vol. 14, page

162). So it can also be said that the t.r. is a theory of the space-time relations of matter in motion. The most important theoretically-ascertained principles of the t.r. are 1. confirmation of the teaching of dialectical materialism on space and time as being forms of the existence of matter. . . . 5. the t.r. by establishing the connection between space and time, and the structure of space-time and matter etc., confirms the teaching of dialectical materialism on the reciprocal connection and interdependence of all aspects of material reality. By posing concrete problems of the dialectics of form and content, concrete and abstract, absolute and relative, their properties and relational phenomena, the t.r. confirms Engels' postulate that natural science is the touchstone of dialectics." [4]

As we have seen, in Stalin's time there was neglect and criticism even of the physical side of the relativity theory ("there is no foundation for the belief that the analysis of space-time made by Einstein is definitive and exhaustive. What is needed is a critical materialistic analysis of the t.r."), while the full fury of their wrath was reserved by the Moscow thunder-bearers for "bourgeois reactionary" philosophers and Einstein himself, who had "helped" them to "exploit" the collapse of the old concepts of space and time.

Under Khrushchev all the neglect and criticism of the theory of relativity was swept away; but, to be on the safe side, no mention was made of any exploitation by anyone of the relativity theory, and thus there were no objections to Einstein's philosophical views. This repre-

4. Bolshaya Sovetskaya Enciklopedia, second ed., Moscow, Vol. 31, p. 411.

sented a substantial change, certainly a very significant one from the point of view of the liberation of scientific thought from the strait jacket of dogma. But it was more of an emergency expedient than the result of a genuine, impartial realization of the truth. Even then, as in Stalin's day, lively efforts were made to ensure that the general "principles" of the relativity theory "served to confirm the doctrines of dialectical materialism," and during this time, under Khrushchev, the quotations used in the proofs were from Lenin instead of Stalin—obviously in line with the back-to-Lenin course. But the actual proofs were nothing more than an arbitrary muddle or, in some instances, deliberate humbug. The "profound criticism" of Newton's views fabricated by Engels and particularly the quotations from his thoughts on the exclusive existence of relative motion are supposed to be a build-up for him as nothing more or less than Einstein's precursor! Between Engels' quoted thought and Einstein's theory, however, there is only one thing in common: the adjective "relative." Engels was simply stressing the trite fact that movement of a body always takes place in relation to another body, while in the relativity theory, as we have seen, the distinction between mass and energy is dispensed with, a fourth dimension in a world of happening is revealed, there is a welding of space and time into space-time, time is treated as relative during the transition into the next co-ordinate system, and so on.

What, in heaven's name, then, is the meaning of that "profound" Engels-Lenin maxim that time and space are aspects of the existence of matter? No meaning except this: that no matter exists which does not possess extension and which does not persist. This is very stale, and very trite. But the Communist is fascinated and bewildered by "forms of existence": it sounds scholarly, profound, and, most important, Hegelian. No more convincing are the attempts to cast Einstein's theory in a mold of Lenin quotations: the Soviet theoretician cites Lenin's notion—another of those eternal truths that sound so profound—that "matter cannot move except in space and time," and he embroiders it: "So it can also be said that the t.r. is a theory of the space-time relations of matter in motion." Where is the logic or intellectual integrity of this? And what megalomaniac, grandiloquent muddle is this: "the properties of space and time constitute the laws and properties of the general structure of the material connections of objects and phenomena"? What good fortune for Soviet science and the Soviet people that proofs like these are not kept secret, that a thinker like this is not kept in the background!

VII

A rational and conscientious observer ought to be able to ferret out the origins of Communism's present ideological degeneration—by examining the various ways in which its great dogmatists and founders conceived of dialectical materialism, developed it, and made use of it. But the strained and violent efforts to force the imaginative potentialities of modern science into the dialectical mold are not the sole, or the latest, aspect of the crisis in the Marxist view of the world. Actually, the crisis is intrinsic, and was present at the very birth of Marxism.

However much Marx himself may have believed in his scientific approach, and he was in fact a social scientist, he was unable to eliminate one essential attribute of his thinking: that it, like all human thinking, realizes only itself in realities. In attaching his views to the workers' movement, he was unable to stop their being systematized, otherwise they would not have been comprehensible, let alone acceptable, as a program for action. The results of his research into the inadequacy and obsolescence of all comprehensive philosophic systems were finally sacrificed to his ambition to actualize his own ideas—to the needs of the socialist movement. Although it is impossible to divorce the revolutionary from the scientist in Marx's versatile and talented personality, his beginnings were as a revolutionary, and it was as such that he sought confirmation in science for his beliefs. In the same way that some people become Communists before they learn Communist theory, so Marx became a Communist first and founded Communist doctrine afterward. That was the sort of man he was; and in his later years he remained, until his death in 1883, the revolutionary who had searched the British Museum for objective laws that would justify his prophetic zeal, that would support a lifework that was inexhaustible because it was directed toward a final liberation from tyranny and exploitation. Such an idealistic and absolute aim had inevitably to override the means, however scientific they might have been, of carrying out the aim. The crisis of Marxism, to adopt the dialectical method here, was to be found in its embryo, and was to be determined by the manner of its inception and by its objective.

Its further course led, in broad terms, to a strengthening of the dogma in its practical application in the socialist movement, but at the same time to a diminution of its scientific character and to an increasingly unbridled intolerance. Engels systematized Marx's views into a doctrine, into a socialist-party philosophy. Then Lenin enriched the philosophy with his theory of revolution and new power, for which he devised an instrument—a revolutionary party of a new kind, and it was this party that Stalin was to reduce to the ways and means of spiritual enslavement. Stalin's reign of terror in the party itself, and the vast gulf that gradually opened between the reality and the theory of Communism, have compelled the present East European leaders not only to abandon dialectics, but also to employ Marxism-Leninism as a weapon in a game of bargainings and concessions. Their own great teachers are only remembered now during celebrations or on those occasions when their own disillusioned forces need to be rallied against "alien ideas." With the nationalization of the Communist parties, the second half of the term Marxism-Leninism is gradually disappearing from currency, so that today it rarely occurs except when the ideological supremacy of Moscow is being underlined. C. L. Sulzberger, after a visit to Tito in mid-May 1968, observed that Tito no longer used the term Leninism. The Czech Communist Cestimir Cizarz made a bold claim that provoked the wrath and repugnance of *Pravda*'s ideologists when he said that "one cannot help noticing certain adverse aspects of attempts to proclaim Soviet Communist experiences as the only possible line for Marxist politics and sometimes to apply Leninism as a monopolistic interpretation of Marxism." [1]

The departure first from Stalin and now from Lenin is in reality a departure from Marx and Marxism. This gives impetus to Mao Tse-tung's hunt for renegades among the East European, Italian, and French Communist party leaders, while at the same time, after witnessing Soviet failures in building a "classless society," Mao is suppressing his own party bureaucracy and elevating

1. *Politika*, Belgrade, June 16, 1968, p. 2.

Marxism combined with his own views to the level of a "new" religion.

There may be some justification for a rejoinder that the greater part of what I am exposing here to criticism is only one side of Marxism, one Marxian feature, or, as is the most frequent charge these days among East European leaders, Stalin's particular distortion of Marxism. But what cannot be disputed is that Marxist thinking and Marxism came to realization solely because of their dogmatism, because of their despotic countenance, which reached a culmination in Stalin and the power structure and economic system he built up. All of Marxism's other features—the humanistic, democratic, non-ideological ones—have survived in the minds of Communist heretics only as illusions, useful perhaps for breaking out of the dogmatic strait jacket, but irrelevant, unrealistic, and ineffectual for activating a different socialist, democratic environment. Those people (like Professor Predrag Vranicki, in Yugoslavia) who condemn me for identifying Communism with Stalinism betray themselves as being incapable of advancing beyond the criticisms of Stalin, and the reforms of Stalinism, made earlier by Communist politicians like Khrushchev and Tito. Views like this often embellish the programs of post-Stalinist Communism (such as Tito's "self-management," Khrushchev's "People's State," or Brezhnev's "scientific leadership"), presenting them as socialism's return to the right road. As a matter of fact, the crisis in Stalinism, precisely because it is primarily a crisis in Communism as a practical reality, cannot be otherwise than a crisis in Communism, and therefore a crisis in Marxism, as an ideology. It seems to me that anyone who fails to realize this will be unable to see the depth of the present crisis in Communism and will, if he is involved, be unable to seek any alternative to it.

Scientific doubt (and perhaps lack of time) prevented Marx from formulating his views and beliefs into a philosophical system. But Marx not only failed to prevent Engels from doing so, he actually encouraged him: he made a critical examination of Engels' *Anti-Dühring*, and wrote its tenth chapter. No wonder! The dogmatism of Marx's materialism, and the dialecticism of his own views, provided the framework and substance of his whole system. After all, he wrote in his most mature, most scientific work, *Capital*, "And so I have frankly admitted that I am the disciple of that great thinker [Hegel], and in the chapter on the theory of value I have, here and there, even toyed with the use of his terminology. The mystification which the dialectic undergoes in Hegel's hands does not in the least disprove the fact that he was the first to work out the general forms of its movement in a comprehensive and conscious way. . . . Indeed, it is easier to get to the heart of religious obscurantism by means of analysis than, vice-versa, to extract from a given, determined set of actual living conditions their religious idealized forms." In a literal sense, Marx did not finally express the whole of his own philosophy, his own ideology; but it was from him, and only from him, that the completed—dogmatized—philosophy could have been extracted, if it was to be put into practice, as it has been. But it is precisely on the basis of this noncommitted attitude that today's "saviors" and "restorers" of Marxism offer us an "embellished" Marxist ideology instead of the "Engelsite" and "Leninist" one, a structure that is more consistent—and inevitably a more egalitarian, more cheerless, and more dogmatic socialism. Fortunately, all this goes on in their own heads, especially among groups of young people who are exasperated because of the failure to achieve the long-desired dream of brotherhood and equality—Communism. Such, then, is the ridiculous pass to which the state of the world has brought us: the "restorers" of Marx try to prove that Marxist ideology is not Marx's, and I try to prove that Marx was a dialectical materialist!

Once the philosophy had been built up as being "scientific," it began with increasing recklessness to emphasize its scientific aspect. It made appeals to the latest scientific discoveries in a tireless endeavor to exploit them for evidence in support of its own validity and to squeeze them into its particular dialectical mold.

It makes no difference that, in line with Marx's remark that "philosophy . . . has only interpreted the world in various ways, while the problem is to change it," [2] Engels, who was aware of the complexity and variety of the natural world as revealed by science, put forward this argument: "But this conception [Marxist historical materialism] brings philosophy to an end in the area of history, in the same way that the dialectical conception of nature makes any philosophy of nature unnecessary and impossible. The problem is no longer one of devising interconnections for phenomena in one's

2. "Theses on Feuerbach," in Selected Works of K. Marx and F. Engels, Belgrade, 1949, Vol. I, p. 393.

own mind but of discovering them in the actual world. Philosophy, having been banished from nature and history, is now left only with the kingdom of pure thought, insofar as such a thing still remains: the science of the laws of the actual process of thought, logic, and dialectics." [3] And, further: "As soon as a specific demand is made upon a science to determine clearly its particular place in the general scheme of things and knowledge about things, every science of such a general scheme becomes superfluous. What then remains self-contained out of the whole range of philosophy to date is the science of thought and the science of the laws of thought,— formal logic and dialectics. Everything else is transferred to the positive science of nature and history." [4] Thus Engels lured himself and others into the trap that was set by their need to be scientific.

This standpoint taken by Engels, or, rather, first by Marx, had its origins in the scientific climate of the time. Many thinkers and scientists (Ernst Haeckel, for instance, and even Ludwig Feuerbach, Marx's materialist predecessor, and, before him, Paul d'Holbach) had realized that there was no basis for any all-embracing philosophical system. Besides, it was one thing to state something, but quite another to do it; and Engels was neither willing nor able to adapt this point of view to the doctrines of his friend Marx; this would have meant that both of them would have had to renounce ideological

3. "Ludwig Feuerbach and the End of Classical German Philosophy," in *Selected Works of K. Marx and F. Engels,* 1950, Vol. II, pp. 388–389.
4. *Anti-Dühring,* Belgrade, 1955, p. 33.

supremacy in the socialist movements and thereby abandon, consequently, their own places in history. Not by accident, Engels introduced the new term "historical materialism." Also not accidentally, the schematization of Marx's doctrine was to be executed in revolutionary Russia: Plekhanov introduced the term "dialectical materialism," the "law" of which Lenin placed at the top of the new faith, the faith in which Stalin proceeded to liquidate millions of "alien elements" and thousands of "deviationists."

Thus, by this synthesis, by this historical sequence, the unification of "Germanic" dogmatism and "Russian" mysticism, Marxist philosophy took on a definite formula with the slogan: "dialectical and historical materialism"—a slogan absurd as such because the second part of it means only application of the first part to human history, and the first part of it is based on the postulate that each phenomenon is historical. Rejecting all philosophical systems, Engels arrogated to himself and Marx one that was new only in that it deposited dialectics alongside formal logic.

This Marxist position has never been properly explained even to this day. Did Engels regard dialectics as, in addition to logic, still another science of human thought? Was it a new dialectical logic? Or its "higher stage"? Many Marxists have pondered worriedly over this, usually coming to the conclusion that formal logic can remain "valid" as the science of the forms of thought founded by Aristotle, whereas dialectics is itself a broader concept. Dialectics would become the science of the laws that, together with the natural world and society, are common to thought, or that, as a reflection of these, have entered into thought. "Because," Engels said in *Anti-Dühring*, "dialectics is nothing more than the science of the general laws of motion and of development in nature, human society and thought." In the same way that Engels banished Hegel's dialectic from the natural world in order to introduce his own dialectic there, so he evicted other philosophies from the incomplete structure of Marxian doctrine in order to settle his own philosophy there, thus making it at the same time Marx's revelation and curse.

But no one has so far succeeded, and no one ever will, in adding a single new feature to the "science" (dialectics) since Marx and Engels, since Hegel, in fact, because in the hands of Marx and Engels it was a scientific instrument of thought based on the nature of being itself. The same is true of the Marxian conception of matter. It is still resident more or less in the eighteenth century, with Diderot and d'Holbach. Many thousands of books have been published in which Marxist professors and evangelists of all kinds have for a whole century been ruminating these problems without furnishing a single innovation to the concept of matter, to Aristotelian logic, or to Hegelian dialectics—indeed, many have succeeded only in impoverishing them. The hopes that materialist dialectics would develop further have come to nothing. Actually, understanding of matter has been further developed by "idealist" scientists, and formal logic has been enriched by the "bourgeois" philosophers, like those in the philosophical school of logical analysis, headed by Bertrand Russell, Ludwig Wittgenstein, and G. E. Moore.

This was inevitable, because the fund of Marxian theories was formulated into a philosophical system, dialectical materialism, in spite of Engels' insistence that "it was not a philosophy at all, but simply a view of the world to be verified and confirmed [and he was certain in advance that it would be so confirmed] in the exact sciences, not in some separate science of the sciences." [5] But it was also inevitable because of the needs of the workers' socialist movements in which Marx and Engels were taking an active part—they were the most important founding members of the International Association of Workers, known as the First International. As spokesmen for the industrial class during the technical revolution, they needed for the coming struggle an ideology with foundations that could be provided only by a new "scientific" philosophy.

There is some justification in the observation that Marxism is not a science in the sense of its being one of the exact sciences, but primarily a social science and a course of action based on its own findings, so that as such it cannot help containing modifications, inaccuracies, and improvisations. Agreed. But then, contemporary Marxists ought to cease their chanting and drum-beating about dialectics as a science, about Marxism as a scientific view of the world, about Marx's ultimate discovery of the laws of society—and, no less, the control of society on the basis of this "science," these "scientific theo-

5. *Ibid.,* p. 164.

ries," these "laws." It would take a real linguistic casuist, or an astute scholastic, to find any difference between a "view of the world" and a "philosophy," even if we dispense with the universally valid dialectic which is an inseparable part of a view of the world in Marxist terms. All educated people, not just the Marxist novices, conceive of Marxism simply and solely as a particular philosophy, in spite of the fact that the post-Engels promoters of Marxism rarely refer to it in those terms: they call it "the dialectical method," "dialectical materialism" (Lenin and Stalin), "Marxist philosophy," "the complete system of proletarian ideology" (Mao Tse-tung). Whatever the terminology that is employed to describe their view of the world, the definitions I have just quoted make it abundantly clear that they cannot mean anything other than a particular philosophy or philosophical system. And the reason for their unwillingness to use the term "philosophy" to denote their way of thinking is to be found in their own uneasy consciences, since, as they well know, the term conceals a measure of the unscientific which they cannot and must not admit.

From the historical point of view, Marxism is the last complete philosophical system to be formulated, in spite of its having declared the end of philosophy as a "science of the sciences." Since Hegel there have been important philosopher-thinkers in certain individual areas or even in several areas, but there has not been a single one who would attempt the discovery of universal laws, i.e., laws equally valid for nature, society, and human thought. No great post-Hegelian philosopher can be said to have been the founder of a comprehensive and impregnable system. Nietzsche is more often a tragic contemplative poet than a philosopher; William James refutes all philosophy by insisting that the value of philosophizing lies solely in its pragmatism; Bergson's subtle analyses deal with biology and art; Russell mainly inquires into human thought and studies society. Only Marxism has been transformed into a complete and also closed philosophical system—all the more closed because it has been inseparable from the struggle for power and from the exercise of power itself. Herein lies the vulnerability of Marxism as a system: as it has become more and more dogmatic, so it has increased its plaintive appeals to science; while science, for its part, has willy-nilly rejected them. The result is that the movement which Marxism inspired, and whose perspectives it illuminated, continues to diverge from Marxism and to obscure its own practical problems.

It is important for classification purposes to note that when Communists refer to their philosophical and political views as a whole, they do not employ the term "Marxist philosophy" or "dialectical materialism." Rather, they use the word "ideology" and various phrases derived from it, such as "socialist ideology," "Communist ideology," "proletarian ideology," "ideological views," "ideological work," and "ideological deviation."

It is instructive to note the origins and development of the term "ideology." It was coined by Destutt de Tracy in 1796 to denote the science of ideas, and later popularized by Napoleon, who sarcastically dubbed the group around Tracy "ideologists." Marx and Engels

then employed it to denote the region of social ideas—
"morals, religion, metaphysics, and other ideology." [6]
And finally Marx included this range under the term:
"juridical, political, religious, artistic, or philosophical
features, in short . . . ideological features." [7] Marx's
attribution of these connotations to the term "ideology"
came from the nature of his social views, which envisaged a whole superstructure of society resting on his material "base." "The social, political, and intellectual life
process, generally, is conditioned by the mode of production of material life. It is not men's consciousness
that determines their social being, but, to the contrary,
their social being that determines their consciousness." [8]
And since "the history of every hitherto-existing society
is the history of class struggles," [9] another of Marx's
maxims is in place here: "The thoughts of the ruling
class are the ruling thoughts in every age, viz., the class
that is the ruling *material* power in society is at the same
time its ruling *intellectual* power." [10]

In using the term "ideology" to denote the total mental activity of the ruling class, usually the bourgeoisie,
Marx does not appear to have been trying to create an
ideology of the oppressed class, the proletariat; that was
what Engels' and Marx's successors did, constructing in

6. *The German Ideology*, Belgrade, 1964, Vol. I, p. 23.
7. *A Contribution to the Critique of Political Economy* in *Selected
Works of K. Marx and F. Engels*, Vol. I, p. 338.
8. *Ibid.*
9. K. Marx and F. Engels, *Manifesto of the Communist Party*, Belgrade, 1948, p. 15.
10. *The German Ideology*, Vol. I, p. 47.

fact a party ideology. According to Marx, every ideology is a group or class ideology and, as such, unscientific. That is why—to be sure, when he was young—he considered ideology as distorted consciousness: "Consciousness can never be anything but a conscious being, and the being of men is their real life process. If in every ideology men and their relationships appear to be upside down, as in the camera obscura, that is because it is a phenomenon resulting from the historical process of their life, in the same way that the upside-down position of objects on the retina of the eye is the result of the directly physical process of life." [11]

These adolescent, Hegelianly intricate views were expressed tentatively by Marx; but, since they are his views, what a pity that all that remains of them as the warp and woof of "proletarian" party ideology are his materialism and the Hegelian dialectic! For if ideology is the mental sum total of a class, group, or stratum, it cannot be created by an individual or organized group. It can only come to fruition in a long, more or less spontaneous, process. But it is possible to construct doctrines, programs, a tactical approach—the ideology of a movement—and that is what Marx and Marxism actually did. Groping toward a scientific approach, and having founded one science, that being sociology, Marx just could not help constructing an ideology, for the simple reason that he was a revolutionary fighter and a visionary.

Later, there was a shift in the meaning of the term

11. K. Marx and F. Engels, *Early Writings,* Zagreb, 1953, p. 293.

"ideology," and some slight modification, in the same way that Communism in practice and theory changed after Marx, but without rupturing intellectual affinity with him. Today the term "ideology" has not the same meaning that Marx attached to it—all forms of the mental activity of a class. Today it means what those forms of activity should have in common—political and philosophical ideas. And although Communist theoreticians are aware that the terms "philosophy" and "ideology" are not identical in derivation, their all-too-frequent preference for the latter is not accidental; even Communists ignorant of the exact meaning of the term "ideology" have an infallible sense for it, since "ideological unity" is part of their way of life, and "ideation," the "ideological struggle," and so on are in fact intellectual aspects of their domination of society. Furthermore, the same or a similar meaning of the term "ideology" has been forced by the Communists upon their opponents, so that it has been said for a long time now that all nations are rent by all sorts of ideologies, while all sorts of ideologists, in their eagerness to make people happy, are at work bamboozling them.

Over and above this, it should not be forgotten that until recently Communism was making the claim, which has still not been withdrawn, to be the *only* world ideology. As a matter of fact, it has been a world ideology from the beginning. It proclaimed itself the movement for proletarians and all the oppressed peoples of the world, and its own Marxist philosophy to be a unique scientific one, which is to say, a universal view of nature and method of human thought, especially in society, where it alone has wrought transformations unparalleled in human history.

We shall not be far wrong if we come to the conclusion that Marxist philosophy is the only philosophy in human history that has served as the substance and framework of an ideology in the present-day meaning of the term: determined ideational viewpoints and the activity of those who adhere to them in all—or, rather, over all—forms of intellectual life in society. We must not be deceived by similarities between the role of Communist philosophy, or ideology, on the one hand, and medieval Christianity, or Confucianism in China, or Brahmanism in India, on the other. There is an essential difference. The difference is this: although social and political groups interpreted the religious doctrines in order to exploit them for their own ends, the doctrines themselves always belonged to diverse groups, frequently at odds with each other, and yet the religious doctrines have survived a variety of social systems, in some cases with little or no adaptation. Marxist ideology and the Communists, to the contrary, have taken care not to be sold short in their intellectual supremacy; by maintaining that the disappearance of social groups is inevitable, and by arrogating to themselves the right to abolish all social distinctions, they have gained a monopoly in the interpretation and production of ideas—all with a clear conscience.

How could it be otherwise when the Communists claim to be the recipients of the revelation of the dialectical-materialist laws governing nature and man?

How could they think or act otherwise when they have been named by a higher power, which they call history, to establish the Kingdom of Heaven in this sinful world to reign over weak human creatures? Luther believed that the sinless man would have no need of laws, while Calvin tried to create such a man by force. The Communists would be in the right if their sinless, *i.e.*, "classless," society were possible, and if they could possess exhaustive knowledge of the laws of society and history and drive the living social reality along in accordance with these laws. But perhaps it is as well that the perfect Communist society is no more a possibility than Luther's sinless man—for with sinful men and unperfect societies we can be sure of not sinking into apathy and we can continue to be creative human beings.

PART TWO

FREEDOM
AND OWNERSHIP

I

Perhaps the most famous passage in which Marx expounds his view of society and human history is this one:

"In the social production of their lives, men enter into certain definite relationships, indispensable to them and independent of their will: these are the relationships of production, which correspond to a specific stage in the development of their material productive forces. The sum total of these relationships of production constitutes the economic structure of society, the real foundation upon which the juridical and political superstructure rises, and to which specific forms of social consciousness correspond. It is the mode of production in material life that determines the general process of men's social, political, and intellectual life. It is not men's consciousness that determines their being; on the contrary, it is their social being that determines their consciousness. At a certain stage in their development, the material productive forces of society come into conflict with the existing relationships of production or—which is only a legal term for the same thing—with the property relationships within which they have hitherto been at work. These relationships become transformed from developmental forms of the productive forces into their fetters. Then begins an epoch of social revolution. With the change in the economic foundation, the whole of the giant superstructure is with greater or less rapidity also transformed. In any consideration of such transformations a distinction should always be drawn between the material transformation of the economic conditions of production, which can be defined with precision by natural science, and the juridical, political, religious, aesthetic, or philosophical transformations, in short, the ideological forms in which men become conscious of the conflict and fight it out. Just as our judgment of an individual is not based on what he thinks of himself, so our judgment of such a period of transformation cannot be based on its own consciousness; on the contrary, we have to explain this consciousness from the contradictions of material life, from the conflict existing between the social productive forces and the relationships of production. No social structure ever perishes before all the productive forces for which it has room have developed; and new, higher relationships of production never appear before the material conditions for their existence have formed in the womb of the old society itself. And so mankind sets itself only the tasks it is capable of carrying out; since, on more close examination, it will always be found that the task itself arises only when the material conditions for carrying it out already exist or are at least in the process of formation. In broad outline, the Asiatic, ancient, feudal, and modern bourgeois modes of production can be designated as progressive epochs in the economic formation of society. The bourgeois relationships of production are the last antagonistic form of the social process of production—antagonistic not in the sense of individual antagonism but in the sense of its arising out of the social living conditions of individuals; while at the same time the productive forces developing in the womb of bourgeois society create the material conditions for resolving that antagonism. Thus with this social formation the prehistory of human society comes to its close." [1]

All Marxists regard this statement as a model of the application of dialectical materialism to human history, a model formulation of historical materialism. Moreover, it could be said that it contains Marx's most important "scientific discovery" (as the Marxists call it) or the epitome of his social philosophy (as others would call it). As far as the role it has played, and continues to play, in human affairs is concerned, the only views that can stand comparison with it are those embodied in the teachings of the founders of the great world religions— Buddha, Christ, and Mohammed.

This passage, and its dramatic standpoint, made things

1. Introduction to *A Contribution to the Critique of Political Economy*, in *Selected Works of K. Marx and F. Engels*, Vol. I, pp. 337–339.

awkward for me in my efforts to emancipate myself from the authority of the Marxist outline of society. My discomfort was increased because the whole question of my remaining steadfast to my own ideas depended to a large extent on whether I abandoned or maintained the views expressed in that particular passage. I must add, at the risk of being accused of mysticism by most of my Communist readers, that for a long time I had had an intuitive feeling about the weak sides of this particular Marxian exposition, but I was unable to set it out in rational terms until the coming of a "revelation" during one of my walks. I have by now lost account of the year and the time of year in which this happened, lost it in that monotonous and endless rotation of days and nights, and I do not know whether it happened during a morning or an afternoon walk; but I do remember the change in the weather, with the clouds scudding from west to east, leaving clear patches behind them. It took place behind the former prison chapel, which had become the Hall of Culture under the new regime, below "the five lindens," as I called the promenade that had been improvised for me by that group of old convicts—along "Djilas's Walk," as the other prisoners called it in their secret whisperings. Embittered, I was still swimming out of the nightmares that tortured and constricted me at nighttime or in the afternoons, when all at once it became clear to me, with the incontrovertible certainty of a feeling, rather than of reasoning, that it is not true that society and the individual—and more paricularly thought—are dependent exclusively upon material forces. Moreover, I realized that no standard measure of such dependence could ever be found, since it will always vary with the actual circumstances, all of which are self-contained and brought about by the action of variable living forces and can never be the same in any two individuals, since man is a rational, creative being as well as merely a living creature. And the "conscious," ideological "edification" of a particular society as undertaken by the Communists, or as they think they have undertaken it—is this not in itself contrary to Marx's thesis that "the mode of production in material life . . . determines the general process of men's social, political, and intellectual life"? And is not the Communist system in itself the most extreme example of how, contrary to Marx, the juridical and political superstructure determines "the relationships of production," "the economic structure of society"? And, finally, in my own life, what were the material conditions or causes that drove me in particular to hurl myself from the comfortable heights of power into the abyss of desolate alienation and prison humiliations? Why should I have cudgeled my brains over the harshness of totalitarian rule, only to spend my declining years scrubbing floors and carrying slops in prison?

But neither in those moments, although excited by my enlightenment, nor later in cold analytic mood did I come to the conclusion that the views of Marx quoted above should be jettisoned irrevocably and *in toto*, nor do I take such a view today in this carefully considered appraisal. On the contrary, Marx's "rational core," *i.e.,* his perception of the economic factor as being vital for society and human thought, is among the most important truths of mankind and is accepted even by scholars who do not agree with Marx generally; and it forms a basis for *all* workable policies today. In this sense men have always been Marxists, in the same way that they could always think logically even before Aristotle invented syllogistic logic. They have known certainly, since Marx's teaching, if not before, that they are "economic" men; just as they have since Aristotle's time known that they are men capable of logical reasoning. It could be added here that none of the Communists' troubles, and none of other people's troubles with the Communists, arises out of the Communists' lust for power, but because they, in spite of Marx's teachings and in spite of their own best intentions, tailored the economy and social relationships to suit their own ideas—"scientific" ideas, of course—and so they were bound to fail. In the last analysis, the economic forces prove to be uncontrollable, and human beings prove to be immutable even given their proneness to yield to brute force and tyranny.

Marx, in fact, has suffered the same fate as other great thinkers. Having arrived at a truth—man's economic dependence—he turned that truth into *the* truth about man. Being aware of the static nature of every formulation, he avoided making formulations. Nevertheless, with his antecedent conviction that his own views were irrefutably scientific, and his work exclusively so, he presented his social-research findings, drawn from history and European society (particularly from the English society of the first half and middle of the nineteenth century) as a discovery of laws that operate "with the inexorability of some natural process."

Poets and sages have commonly expressed the notions

of the transitoriness of empires, and of the commitment of man to toil and struggle, and of his striving through historical and other researches to make important discoveries about the world. It is known that ever since men became aware of the deficiences in virgin nature and the inadequacies of their own aboriginal consanguineous communities, all societies had survived until the emergence of new forms, new prerequisites for survival. Continually, they have passed through struggles with various conflicting forces—class, caste, rank, group, and so on—to which they were driven by religious, philosophical, and all kinds of other ideas and lured on by pictures of the fruits to be won by struggle. These intimations were confirmed in Marx's time by vivid recollections of the still-smoldering conflicts of the French Revolution, the greatest and most multifarious revolution in a nation that was hitherto the most powerful and civilized in modern history. These intimations were, moreover, augmented by the relentless and increasingly stark division of the newly formed European industrial society into two groups: the owners of the means of production—the capitalists—and the owners of the labor force—the proletarians. Marx's mind, insatiable and visionary but obsessed with dialectics and the applications of science, made further advances in ascertainments and beliefs: he discovered that societies decline and rise as a result of a struggle for new relationships in production, and from this he made the generalization that human history hitherto was the history of class struggle; he discovered the decline of civilizations, and generalized that as progress; he discovered the productive forces (the means of production plus men inured to labor) as the material driving force, and he generalized these as the basis of all social aspirations and human thought; he discovered that further development of the productive forces would lead to the disappearance of private capitalist ownership and the appearance of collective socialist ownership, but he envisaged his own future society as being nonantagonistic, free from all those limitations and adversities he had noted in earlier societies and analyzed in capitalist society with such incomparable persuasion and animation.

His analyses are undeniably the result of toil and sacrifice such as might be envied by the most dogged and passionate scientists, but he came to the fundamental ideas I have mentioned, and to his vision of the future, on the basis of his preconceived beliefs. He had for a long time been a Hegelian dialectician and a materialist monist, and he had just discovered the "ultimate" dialectical-materialist "laws" of society and thought. His most scientific and important work, *Capital,* was written after he had reached his mature years. Here he based his case, which he presented with razor-sharp conviction, on evidence he had ransacked from almost the whole of world literature in the fields of economics and history, a task that could only have been undertaken in the British Museum. It is an achievement whose grandeur, complexity, and fervor have seldom been surpassed in the history of the human spirit. But even in this work he was doing nothing, in essence, but establishing the "absolute truth" of the faith that had been revealed to him in his youth: "Since Communism means the positive abolition of *private property as being man's self-alienation,* and since this is a genuine *appropriation of man's essence* by man, Communism is the complete return of man to himself as a *social* (i.e., human) being, a return that is newborn as a conscious act and accomplished within the total wealth of previous development. . . . It is the solution to the riddle of history, and it is aware that it is the solution." [2]

Marx made his faith more persuasive by means of his scientific approach, but he was unable to make it a science. The scientific in him was an embryonic faith and ideology, and in time it became a creed demonstrated by science. Consequently, Marx's "science" and thus his doctrine do not merit anything like as much respect and admiration as does their founder.

Had his analyses and inferences not been *a priori,* had they been less categorical, had there been fewer "discoveries" and more description, Marx would perhaps occupy a much greater place in science, but it would still not be nearly so great as the one he occupies in modern history, for desperate and disenfranchised people and nations would not have gathered around relative, unabsolute, and not very hopeful truths. Be that as it may, mankind will be grateful to Marx for having enlarged the knowledge of human destiny, and he will have his place in history among the great visionaries and revolutionaries. But to this day history is not in any way capable of being interpreted—and can only marginally be made—with the aid of his doctrines: in actual history,

2. *Economic and Philosophic Manuscripts of 1844,* in K. Marx and F. Engels, *Early Works,* Zagreb, 1967, p. 275.

141

in the world of reality, there are no such schematic and sharp divisions between the "base" (*i.e.*, the relationships of production and the productive forces) and the superstructure (*i.e.*, ideas, institutions, and organizations), nor does the former unconditionally and without residue determine the latter.

I have already suggested that the Communist system itself, with its ideological economy,[3] provides the most forthright and convincing refutation of Marx's thesis on the conditioning of the superstructure by the base. The fact that one hundred and twenty-five years have now passed since Marx formulated his thesis is not something to be dismissed lightly; but none of the dissertations on historical, sociological, or philosophical subjects based on Marx's economic and class categories (and thousands, if not hundreds of thousands, have been written) has succeeded in proving itself of lasting value—in the same way that no major scientific work has been based on any religious doctrine.

The changes in relationships among men—in other words, history as a series of events—take place with the participation of all the forces, both material and intellectual, with now one group playing the dominant role and later another group, and so on. Thus history is in

3. I first used the term "ideological economy" as a title for a chapter in *The New Class.* And although objections may be raised that I overestimated the longer-term possibilities for Communists, by using ideology, to accelerate in an ideological direction the formation, development, and even the very nature of the productive forces, I maintain that the translators of the book blunted the sharpness and meaning of the original title by rendering it as "Dogmatism in the Economy."

essence a group action performed by nations with their lives at stake, and by thinkers who discover the inevitabilities, and by leaders who display clear practicable ideas and organizational abilities. The making of history is a creative act in which it is impossible to isolate, and still less to evaluate, the roles of its various factors. In any case, Marx and Marxism are the best testimony to the tremendous, unambiguous, and occasionally decisive roles played by ideas in history. It may be contended that Marx himself had noticed this when pointing out that ideas when they grip the masses become themselves a material force. Such a contention, however, would not be entirely justified, because in his thesis Marx remains faithful to his schematic division into the material as a base and the mental as its product. With him, ideas become a force only after they have become matter, when they have become accepted by the masses.

Much more important than this is the fact that nations, social strata, and people living today under Communism can no longer adhere uncritically to Marxian doctrines without jeopardizing their viability and their place in the contemporary world—in short, without jeopardizing the development of those same productive forces whose importance in people's lives and in human relationships Marx was the first to point out. The irony is that not only has Communism fallen out with Marx, but also, owing to Marx, it is impossible for a society under Communism to extricate itself from the dead end and absurdities into which it has fallen. I know of no key to history, nor do I believe that one exists; that lock, like every other enigma, has yet to be opened in a new way, with new learning and sacrifices. . . . Heisenberg draws this conclusion from modern physics: "Nature is unpredictable." [4] But it can be objected that that, for heaven's sake, is *nature!* This is the sort of rejoinder that might well be made by power-seekers and dogmatists, convinced, or now pretending to be convinced, that society, people, and human destiny are predictable and therefore pliable. The human mind cannot, normally, help being astonished at such conceit, attributing it, as the only possible explanation, to people's infinite capacity for stupidity and their insatiable lust for domination over others, over society, over human destiny.

No one can interpret the world and contemporary society exclusively in terms of Marxist theory, or any other single theory, without descending to absurdities, or sophisms. If the relationships of production "correspond to a specific stage in the development of their material productive forces," what is the explanation for the fact that in the Soviet Union, where the form of society is presumed to be "higher" than in the United States, the level of the productive forces is—and will for a long time continue to be—considerably lower? If relationships in production vary in West and East, as they obviously do, what is the explanation for the same or similar phenomena in art, in science, among the actions and styles of young people, and so on? If Communist systems today are supposed to be scientifically managed (according to Marx), that should mean the elimination of the antagonisms in the "bourgeois modes

4. Quoted by Arthur Koestler in *The Ghost in the Machine,* London, 1967, p. 17.

144

of production." Then how is it that so many unforeseen economic crises emerge in Communist systems, and why are there social conflicts and a persistent sense of hopelessness? And how is it that notwithstanding different "production relationships" or "property relationships" and the same, or nearly the same, "development levels . . . in the material productive forces," we find similar ideas and similar social phenomena, similar difficulties and similar projects in the economy in a number of both "socialist" countries and "capitalist" countries? There is no end to such questions, to the degree that there is no end to change and disintegration in Communism.

For Communists the issue is no longer a matter of disapproval of heretics and farseeing sages; it is now a matter of the life and sanity of men who, having given their all to the society, seek little more in return than to live honest, useful lives with some sort of security for themselves and their families. Even if the Communist world were "the best of all possible worlds," it would not be able to go on living armed with the "most progressive" "scientific" ideas and with secret police hovering like "guardian angels" over men's spirits. The sciences, modern communications, and the information media have contracted time and space in our perceptions and concepts; technology has demolished monopolies and even destroyed the "advantages" of this or that ideology, and it has, as Marshall McLuhan has shown, transformed the world into a huge village, scattering human existence into outer space.

Today this is not merely obvious; it is also part of everyday human life. Even so, I shall have to dwell on the Marxist (though it is not only Marxist) doctrine of governing laws, the doctrine of the inexorability of progressive development for the human race and individuals.

A complete picture of my reflections here, and an understanding of them, demands that this problem be thoroughly gone over, particularly because social progress is accepted without question in the East and is usually pronounced in the West an irrefutable truth and a sacred duty, while in the name of progress frenzied acts of violence take place and the most extravagant economic features are maintained.

Even if I had a sufficient grasp of biology and astronomy, I would steer quite clear of any controversy on the evolution of living creatures from lower to higher forms, up to man as the highest form, or on the roles of "formless" and "scattered" particles in the origins of celestial bodies. But I am so firmly convinced that the doctrine of the evolutionary character of human society and the human being is, at the very least, unreliable that I cannot help thinking that it must have come to biology and cosmogony from philosophy, from the "scientific" and social beliefs of the nineteenth century about progress as a universal law. Today that is too simple, too "intelligible," to be true.

But now we must return to society.

It really is extraordinary how people living today, most of them contemporaries of the time of Hitler's death factories and Stalin's "labor camps," can be so ready to defend the doctrine that there are laws governing the progress of human beings and human communities, when history knows of no other regimes that have wreaked such unscrupulous vengeance upon whole nations and whole strata of society. Did not the Athenian citizen have more freedom, and the Roman citizen more rights, than are to be found under many regimes of our times? Even if we accept the explanation, or, more accurately, the excuse, that Hitler and Stalin were offshoots of an evil attendant upon declining and, obversely, emerging social orders, none of us has the right to consider the time in which we live, with the shadow of nuclear death over the lives of all human creatures, to be better or more progressive than any previous one. Would it not be wiser, and more honest, to try to understand people and their communities, to approach them without any final and preconceived truths, which is to say, as they are, as they must be, given the circumstances— neither absolutely or ultimately good nor absolutely or ultimately evil?

Knowing is also acting. Upon our understanding of people depends our future relationship toward them. Those who accept progress without any reservations are usually people who are driving others, and the very tide of life around them, toward their own convictions. Tyranny begins with ultimate truths about society and man. And even if every new society in embryo is usually composed of such truths, they become, finally, the hotbeds of that society's putrefaction. There are no ultimate truths about man, any more than there are about the world. The truth about man is boundless and unforeseeable. The truth about man is a continuous but never-the-same expansion of his potentialities in the outside world, a continuous but erratic winning of freedom by man for himself in society.

Perhaps I am wrong from the scientific point of view: perhaps, after all, the human race is not so unfortunately immutable; perhaps over-all, and in the long term, there is progress in human society and in the individual human being. But it is given to no one to determine the speed at which this hypothetical progress takes place, let alone to dispose of the conditions and means for carrying it out. And if such power should be given to anyone, could he be so omniscient and perfect in all things as to be able to make and mold human beings in his own image and remake human institutions according to his whim? Would people consent to this? Are they not as intransigent in freedom and felicity as they are implacable toward oppression and affliction?

But, with all this said, I do not suggest that progress does not exist in technology and the sciences, and still less that I would wish to oppose it. This sort of progress ought to be regarded, and with more justification, it seems to me, as an expansion of the conditions for human survival. Although man is not the only creature unable to survive in a pure, unchanged natural environment, he is certainly the only one whose very survival depends on his ability to change it constantly, to increase his store of knowledge and expand the conditions for his survival.

This, the challenge of making strides into a new environment, into new opportunities, stands in front of people living under Communism, and, in other ways, before the rest of the world. Freedom has never been either a dogma or an abstraction. Today it means the liberation of science and technology from the strait jacket placed on them by systems of ownership and the like, no less than the liberation of human minds and bodies from dogma and tyranny.

II

History does not exactly abound with instances of thinkers' predictions having come true, least of all those relating to social patterns and people's attitudes and ways of life. In this respect, Marx's record is not much better than that of any other thinker before him or since, in spite of the fact that his ideas have spread like fire, and that movements inspired by them have dominated more than one third of the human race. Still more unreal, and still further from realization, are Lenin's prognostications, perhaps precisely because they were more down-to-earth, since he was much less of a philosopher and prophet than was his teacher.

What happened to Lenin's revolution and his Communist (Third) International?

For Lenin, the October Revolution was but one triumph of the world proletariat, a Russian sacrifice in the cause of human freedom. But even during Lenin's lifetime it was turning into a frantic struggle for power, and soon after his death it became a fanatical tyranny which devoured nine tenths of Lenin's confederates, some seven hundred thousand Communist party members, as can be seen now in the official statistics. The ordinary citizens of this "first country of socialism" fell victim to the struggle in such enormous numbers—some say about eight million—that the present rulers do not dare quote a figure, unless, of course, they consider that such people, not being among the "faithful," are unworthy of precise statistics. Today, all that remains of the spirit of the revolution are hackneyed phrases that barely cover the nakedness of sometime revolutionaries and their sons and grandsons, men who have long been transformed into the privileged elite of the party bureaucracy. The duplicity that the bureaucrats employ against their own working class and the various national communities of the Soviet Union and the subordination of foreign revolutionary movements to their own great-power interests are features essential to their livelihood and for their survival. At its inception, the Communist International (the Comintern) was unfree and uninternational. Believing in world revolution, or at least in the unity of the world Communist movement, Lenin himself drew up the conditions for membership in the organization, and in doing so, in spite of his good intentions and all his efforts at the time, he imposed the imprint of his own thinking upon that of foreign socialist theoreticians, and reduced the experiences of foreign Communist parties to by-products of the Russian Bolshevik party. After Lenin, the decisive step was taken by Stalin. He carried out, as far as he was in a position to do so, a radical "purge" of the foreign parties, on the line of that in the Bolshevik party; and he turned the Comintern into a satellite of the Russian-Soviet state and, finally, when it became a hindrance to his own policies of state, he dissolved it (in 1943). Lenin was by now transformed into relics and an icon for the new Russian Orthodox church. These became the object of increasing veneration as the authority of the man behind them, Lenin, declined; and while his books were read with increasing zeal, less and less attention was paid to their contents.

Such is the pass to which Lenin's work and teachings have come. But there is another side to this, a living and practical side that testifies that the world, if not a better place, is not a worse one, although it no longer accepts the Comintern's promise of an end to poverty and wars, and of brotherhood and happiness in the "world dictatorship of the proletariat." The seed of revolution has been sown all over the world—although it has not everywhere fallen on fertile ground or anywhere brought forth the expected fruits—and this is no mean achievement. Even if the world dictatorship of the proletariat was a practical possibility, it would be foolish and disingenuous for one movement or one country, let alone for a single individual, to claim to be the repository of all human wisdom. A more plausible assertion about Lenin's country is that today, under the colorless and amorphous leadership of Brezhnev and Kosygin, it is a happier and more agreeable place, although for a long time now it has dispensed with Lenin's revolutionary heritage. There is today a fall in exports of revolution, but more bread at home, more houses and cars; there is a shortage of revolutionary missionaries, but a greater abundance of men at home to work usefully with their hands and brains. Even arbitrary acts of coercion against its own citizenry are on a much smaller scale today in Russia than in Lenin's time— surely an advance, unless anyone (and such people do exist) considers a revolutionary reign of terror to be the acme of human happiness and freedom.

Lenin not only built up his own power through the revolution, but he also shaped and molded a new society by means of dogma. But there is another side to this: his exclusive hold on the dogma and his revolutionary implacability, though unacceptable today in the unchanged form in which they survive, were in his time a useful expedient; and they have thrust him among the great men of history, making him, perhaps, the most important figure of the twentieth century. This exclusiveness and implacability helped him to seize hold of a new form of power and of society, for Russia and a host of other countries a workable and viable form. Alexander Kerensky attaches great importance to his theory that Lenin was not a Marxist but a Blanquiste; this may be music to the ears of the West European bourgeoisie and it may sound convincing to reformist social democrats, but, even if it were true, it would not detract from Lenin's greatness or from the actual fact of his achievement. Today the laments of P. B. Struve sound even more ridiculous: "Going to the heart of the matter, I can only say of the 1917 revolution and the subsequent years, that as a fact in the life of the nation it was a *great misfortune,* and, as far as they 'made a mistake,' it was a big mistake. . . ." [1] Although ideas, morals, and

1. Quoted in *Mosti,* Munich, 1967, p. 212.

emotions play a significant, and sometimes decisive, role in human struggles, there is nothing more erroneous and futile than to judge a historical event retrospectively on that basis. Whatever has irrevocably happened is unchangeable and irreversible; and Hegel would have been quite right in maintaining that, although every period is too individual for nations to be able to learn from history, nevertheless something can be learned about what ought *not* to be done. . . .

However we may judge Lenin's doctrines and deeds, they are inappropriate to contemporary needs and conditions in the struggle for better living conditions, for human freedom, and for equality among nations. Not only that, but they are the principal weapon of a particular world power, the Soviet Union, for extending its state influence throughout the world and its hegemony over Communist parties and over countries with a Communist government. In this connection, it must be remembered that the disintegration of Communism is not owing only to its organic inability to resolve today's basic problems of life among the nations under its overlordship, but also to its failure to survive in its own closed world. Hence, a critical approach to Lenin's picture of contemporary societies, and also to his methods of struggle and his forms of organization, imposes itself as a prerequisite for any democratic transformations in Communist parties and states, and for their release from the payment of ideological tribute to their conquerors, the Soviet oligarchy.

On top of everything else, Lenin's picture of society

and international relations was not an accurate one even in his own day, except as an ideology for a revolutionary, Communist-oriented movement, applicable only to conditions in Russia, where the people were simply incapable of making strides into a new environment until they had first shaken off the shackles of backwardness, practical servitude, and a surviving feudal autocracy. All later revolutions differed from the October Revolution, in the conditions prevailing and the forces employed and the forms taken, although they all swore allegiance to Lenin and were sheltered behind Leninism.

Thus, as for Lenin in his day, so for every democratic Communist today, every democratic socialist, every fighter for human freedom inside and outside the Communist world, the question is: What is to be done? The answer to that question is not to be—cannot be—found any longer in Lenin.

Lenin's conception of society in his own day is most fully expounded in a slim work, *Imperialism as the Highest Stage of Capitalism,* written in 1916 in Zurich. The material for this discourse was taken mainly from works by two social democrats, John A. Hobson's *Imperialism* and Rudolf Hilferding's *Finance Capital.* But Lenin drew his own revolutionary inferences. It must be said at the start that many of the analyses and inferences in Lenin's sources, particularly in Hobson's book, have proved more accurate than Lenin's own, but since the purpose of my argument is not to make comparisons of achievements and values, but to demonstrate the impracticability of Marxism-Leninism for our own times and the conditions of modern life, I shall make mention only of what manifestly confirms that thesis.[2]

Lenin comes to these conclusions: "If one is to make the shortest possible definition of imperialism, it would be true to say that it is the monopoly stage of capitalism. . . . But excessively short definitions, for all their convenience in summing up the essentials, are nevertheless inadequate. . . . So without forgetting the tentative and relative significance of definitions in general, since they never succeed in embracing the multilateral connections of a phenomenon in its full development, we must construct a definition of imperialism that will include its five basic characteristics: 1) The concentration of production and capital which has reached such a high level of development that it has created monopolies which play a decisive role in economic life; 2) The merging of banking and industrial capital and the establishment, on the basis of this 'finance capital,' of a financial oligarchy; 3) The export of capital, as opposed to the export of goods, which now assumes a very important role; 4) The establishment of international associations of capitalists which share out the world; and 5) The completion of the territorial distribution of the earth by the biggest capitalist states. Imperialism is capitalism at a stage of development when domination by monopoly and finance capital has grown up, when the export of capital has assumed importance, when the international trusts have begun to share out the world, and when the distribution of the

2. I recommend Louis Fischer's study *The Life of Lenin*, New York, 1964. Here, amongst other things, this question is tackled thoroughly and persuasively (pp. 95–107).

whole territory of the earth has been completed by the biggest capitalist countries. . . ." [3] "The conclusion to be drawn from all that has been said above about the economic essence of imperialism is that it is capitalism in transition or, more accurately, on its deathbed." [4]

It is sufficient to plumb the depths in the title of Lenin's discourse, *Imperialism as the Highest Stage of Capitalism,* in order to grasp the extent of his dogmatism at the time as well as the present-day unreality of his inferences. Capitalism, presumably the social order practiced in the United States, the West European countries, and Japan, is obviously thriving and advancing beyond its "highest stage." Capitalism as defined in practice in these countries has advanced because: One, although the concentration of production and capital has continued, and is continuing at an accelerated pace to this day, what is typical of the Western economies are not monopolies as they used to exist in the classic Hilferding-Lenin sense, but what John Kenneth Galbraith calls the "market structure of the industrial system," [5] which means that prices are fixed by the experts and technicians of the big companies, who plan production, investigate markets, and so on. These men are now the main human factors in modern production—both under "capitalism" and under "socialism." It is no accident that Yugoslav economists have been complaining of the "phenomenon of monopoly" ever since the industrial

3. *Imperialism as the Highest Stage of Capitalism,* in V. I. Lenin, *Selected Works,* Belgrade, 1949, Vol. I, Book II, pp. 403–404.
4. *Ibid.,* p. 435.
5. *The New Industrial State,* London, 1968, p. 185.

enterprises began to "fix" prices, so that Galbraith is right in concluding: "Socialist industry also works, as a matter of course, within a framework of controlled prices. In recent times the Soviet Union, following the earlier Yugoslav practice, has been according to firms and industries some of the flexibility in adjusting prices that the more informal evolution has accorded the American system. This has been widely hailed as a return, by these countries, to the market. That is a mirage. It does not mean, any more than in the American system, that the socialist firm is subject to control by market prices over which it exercises no influence. It only means that its control can be more flexibly exercised in response to change." [6] As far back as the days of Theodore Roosevelt, monopolies were prohibited by law in the United States, and after the last war in other countries, too. No one, of course, can maintain that individual companies do not engage in price-cutting, or that big banks and groups of companies never attempt to achieve a monopolistic position. Such ambitions and take-overs are also a feature of "socialist" economies, where, as in Yugoslavia for instance, some sort of free market has emerged. In spite of this, however, it is quite obvious that the present-day economies of the Western countries do not rest solely on combine monopoly, but also on free competition. Two, many states today are "socialist," but the rest of the globe is not divided among "international monopoly associations" or among "the biggest capitalist states," but has, rather, been transformed, leaving aside the colonies of backward Portugal, into independent states for whose

6. *Ibid.*, p. 191.

favors the great powers compete, "capitalist" and "socialist" alike. Three, the export of capital, although it persists on a considerable scale as compared with what it was in the days when Hobson, Hilferding, and Lenin were writing about it or in the period between the two world wars, is incomparably less, both in volume and in importance, than the export of goods. Moreover, what is particularly characteristic is that a larger proportion of capital goes to developed countries than to the underdeveloped world, while the underdeveloped countries, for their part, are doing everything in their power to attract capital. Further, capital is being exported in various guises by both "capitalist" and "socialist" countries, and the former are even beginning to export it to the latter, as to Yugoslavia, for instance.

This is an external picture of the present "capitalist" world, admittedly a sketchy picture, drawn in order to show how out of date Lenin's view is, even in areas where it used to be considered fairly accurate. Some of the blanks have to be filled in. At least we should remember that the colonies achieved their independence not, as Lenin had predicted, as a result of revolutions in the home metropolises combined with rebellions among the subject peoples, but because social and technical changes made the investment of capital more profitable at home—in the developed countries—and made trade brisker and safer with independent countries. This does not mean, of course, that the colonial powers withdrew quietly and gladly from their colonies. Industrial groups and elements who had grown rich on cheap labor and raw materials in the backward areas of the world opposed decolonization with everything in their power, and national-liberation movements sprang up among the subject nations, which soon had their hands on modern weapons and media, so that it was not possible to treat them as feudal vassals to be subdued by sending a couple of gunboats and mercenary punitive expeditions. And whenever and wherever the forces of colonialism were strong and influential, as in France, for instance, in relation to certain of its colonies, an uprising of the subject people forced the metropolitan government to its senses and brought about a change in the balance of forces. Communist resolutions and slogans, in line with Lenin's theories, identify contemporary capitalism with imperialism, and judge the contemporary social order in the West in the light of Lenin's descriptions of imperialism at the beginning of this century. It is no wonder that they give the impression of being grotesque and unreal and are so often the object of derision.

The meaning of this is not that there has never been any imperialism, or that there is no such thing and never will be, if by imperialism we are to understand the oft-practiced snatchings and grabbings of the great powers and the threats of jealousies between them. Nations would be neither powers nor "great" if in one way or another they had not been empires and imperialist. But then it is clear that Lenin's own country, in spite of its fine words and bitter experiences with Yugoslavia in 1948, has still not renounced its policy of subjugating sister Communist countries by ideological and military means. In this respect it is different from China, which is winning its place in the world by means of revolutionary dogmatism, and from the United States, whose privileged position is maintained primarily by superior technology and financial wealth.

When examined from the standpoint of contemporary conditions and knowledge, Lenin's views on "imperialism," and in other areas, suffer from two fundamental and interconnected shortcomings: the doctrinaire approach to factual situations and the effect of unfulfilled prophesies.

Before even starting his analysis of capitalism, Lenin was convinced that its end was near; the abundant statistics and data that were his special passion were to provide the confirmation. And naturally they did provide "confirmation," since his faith, taken from Marx and learned by heart, was unwavering, and it found further evidence in certain industries where monopolistic tendencies and monopoly control were a running sore on the flesh of capitalism. Add to this the decisive influence exerted by monopoly groups on government policy which at that time was evident. So faith and some facts were combined to produce the "logical" conclusion that this was a sign of the "highest stage of capitalism"— of "capitalism on its deathbed." Lenin's conceptions and predictions, taken over-all, showed demonstrable signs of being practicable when applied to such a dependent and underdeveloped capitalism as Russia's, where there was virtually no monopoly or finance capital; but they were doomed to failure in the context of a Western structure precisely because of his confidence in Marx's "scientific laws," because of his conviction that the knell of capitalism was just about to toll. . . . And even today

161

I am among those who believe in the inevitability of that knell, because no society, no civilization, is forever enduring. Furthermore, it seems to me that the decline has set in, the "transformation" already begun in many respects—the nationalization of important industries; the enlargement of community property; the proliferation of state social welfare; progressive taxation; the larger, often key, role, being played by the state in industry; increasingly, workers' wage demands being made in relation to profits, and so on. But with Lenin it was not only a question of the nature of his faith; it was also a matter of specifying the method to be employed. Armed uprising of the working class against the capitalist class was the only "possible," the "inevitable," way of changing all societies, and therefore Western capitalist societies. Furthermore, he specified the form of the government and of society—Marx's dictatorship of the proletariat—and that meant that soviets and complete nationalization of the means of production were "bound to" emerge from the ruins of capitalism. . . . This did not happen in the West, and there is no prospect that it will. Technological development and free forms of ownership have reached a point in the West where the top layer of the working class, if indeed not its main bulk, has been merging into the middle class, the bourgeoisie.[7] This can only mean that that class taken as a whole has *ceased* to be revolutionary in the Marxist-Leninist sense, in the sense that it is fighting for the dictatorship of the prole-

7. Convincing data about this are adduced, for example, in Ralf Dahrendorf's book, mentioned earlier, *Class and Class Conflict in Industrial Society.*

tariat, for the power of the "avant-garde proletariat" (the Communist party) and for nationalization even when it is unnecessary from the point of view of the economy or production. But this does not mean that these Western societies have remained as they were. On the contrary, societies in Western Europe and the society of the United States are, I am firmly convinced, actually moving toward socialism in this way. Theirs is a movement toward a socialism that has no similarity with the socialism that actually exists in the Soviet Union and China today, and certainly not with any model that has been projected by any socialist thinker. The recent student and workers' unrest in France may indicate that the French working class has now set forth on the road taken a long time ago by their comrades in the United States and Western Germany; the anarchist and left-Communist students may have been the "fuse" that detonated the general strike, but the "explosive charge" itself, the workers, was wisely content with an "unideal" pay rise and a greater role in the distribution of profits, leaving their "idealist" firebrands in the lurch. The Eastern type of "socialism," with its dictatorships "in the name of" the working class, has certainly provided experiences to influence this sort of working-class development and conduct in the West. Moreover, fear of Communism and revolution soon jogged the Western powers and propertied classes to the sensible decision to let the workers have "a slice of the national cake" and to get down to a planned control of the economy and reform of social legislation, indeed a reform of society itself. But other causes, deeper and more compelling, were the decisive ones: rapid technical progress, a heritage of political freedom, the Western powers' privileged position as a result of a higher level of development. If anyone sees the changed working-class role in the West as a sign of its lack of class consciousness, as a betrayal of its "historical objectives," that is only evidence that he is ascribing his own dogmas and objectives to the working class. And if anyone finds that these pressures on the West, to make the sort of reforms that Communism is on its own motivation still carrying out, are no more than Satan in a new guise leading the Good Lord to greater justice, that is only evidence for the existence of dogmatism on the opposite side, the anti-Communist side. For people like myself, who have to all intents emancipated themselves from the dogmas of either side, Communist influence in the West and demands for "Western-type" freedoms in the East can be taken as evidence that the world as a whole is shedding its utopian myths and is beginning in various ways to live, think, and create as a world-wide comity of men.

In my estimation, it all goes deeper, and will take longer, than Lenin, in his allegiance to Marx, believed. Capitalist forms of ownership, whether the early forms of private property or the monopolies of recent date or, still further, today's mixed forms, are only a way of life whose roots are older than capitalism. Indeed, they can be found in classical Greek philosophy, in ancient Rome, in Christianity, and in European feudalism. Capitalism as we see it today sprang from a West European environment, and for the most part it grew and gathered strength there, reaching its purest form in the United

States, while in the rest of the world it was mainly an imposition or an import. Consequently, a replacement for this form of ownership in the West can only take place in continuity with the life of the peoples there. In other words, it can be said that the end of capitalism need not mean an end to their way of life for the people of the area, in the same way that the Communist system cannot be replaced except in a way and with forms that will mean the survival, the preservation, of the identity of the people living under Communism today.

III

In view of what has been said, it is not surprising that a myth about the universal and unconditional benefits of the new "socialist" form of ownership was created out of Lenin's belief that capitalist monopoly and monopoly imperialism were the last stage of capitalism, which would usher in the "higher . . . progressive epoch of socio-economic formulation"; and the myth went even further with the belief that this had actually happened in Russia with the October Revolution, and was current even before it had been tried out in practice. . . . I, too, believed in the myth for a long time, right up to when the actual facts and my own intelligence taught me to give the cold shoulder to anything that was justified on purely ideological grounds.

Marxist-Leninist ideas were real and ideal as long as they moved the masses and served to destroy obsolete and reactionary regimes, but they became transformed into dogmas and myths for the self-deluding Communists of today to use in justifying their distorted world of reality. Their argument is that the supposedly prevailing social ownership in their system must inevitably offer greater opportunities for technical advance and social justice than exist, or ever will exist, in other social orders. What they have in mind is the United States, as their principal ideological, social, and military competitor.

This alleged universal and unconditional superiority in the forms of ownership (Marx would call them the "relationships of production") prevailing in all Communist countries is the last and most crucial of the myths of Marxist dogma and Marxism in practice. Like every myth, it is a reflection of some simple truths it once possessed, but it is more; it is still a source of benefit, for the party bureaucracy which emerged from this system of ownership used the myth to climb to power, and it still uses it to keep in power.

In *The New Class* I went in detail into the true character of property and ownership in a Communist system. Now, for the sake of continuity, I am making the point that the Communist form of ownership emerged as a result of the undeveloped character of certain countries (primarily Russia, China, and Yugoslavia) and their inability to carry through an industrial revolution with capitalist private ownership. Like every form of society and ownership in its early stages, the Communist system has represented itself as an ideal, as a society leading to the abolition of class and exploitation, as an all-national form of ownership containing no elements of coercion and injustice, one free from the crises and stagnation inherent in the scramble for profits and for cheap sources of raw material and labor. As usual, things turned out differently in reality: today, Communism suffers from all the ills which it had so justly stigmatized as being the curse of capitalism, and deeper researches into its ownership patterns reveal that the political, party bureaucracy has shattered its own paramount ideal by keeping a monopoly of management and control in its own hands. This monopoly is not, admittedly, complete in all countries—Yugoslavia, for instance, is an exception, though even there it has not been completely abandoned. Thus in Communist countries the party bureaucracy has been concealing under a coating of ostensible probity and legal equivocation its real proprietorial nature, which is grasping and predatory.

And here lie the foundations for the myth of the superiority of the system of ownership which Communism has established and is trying to perpetuate. Here they lie on the natural self and visible role of Communism, which may have been genuine in the past but which are now absolutely involved in their own mystique.

There is a proverb in my country—"No man can tell in what faith he will die." I hope that I never have to be a defender of any capitalist system, and that includes the American system. My particular reason is that in America itself capitalism is already undergoing a change into a system in which, it seems to me, private property is becoming less relevant in the life of the nation, a system which, for all that, will not differ any less in the future than now from the present systems prevailing in the East and which will probably be no less a subject of East-West dispute than at present. That is not the issue. Precisely because I maintain that no system is absolutely and unconditionally superior to other systems, and, further, that systems based on private ownership or party bureaucracy are both unsuitable for the life of people and nations today, I believe that it is the duty of everyone to be a witness for the truth in his own part of the world—to demolish the myths that are a stumbling block to mutual understanding and the creation of a more suitable system of ownership and a more suitable environment for people to live in. That is why, without regard for any accusations or insults I may incur, I have been an advocate of the demolition of myths of the absolute and unconditional superiority of the system of ownership imposed by Communism. I have heretofore avoided quoting any figures, because statistics are a favorite instrument of the Communists, particularly in the Soviet Union, and are used unscrupulously for the sole purpose of presenting, and frequently embellishing, their own successes, while suppressing or distorting successes elsewhere in the world.

This is what a few statistics[1] reveal: coal production in the United States in 1850 was under 10,000,000 tons, and in 1910 was 500,000,000 tons, which means it increased fiftyfold in sixty years; steel production in about 1872 was less than 100,000 long tons and in 1910 more than 25,000,000 long tons, which means it increased by 250 times in thirty-eight years; in 1902, 5,969,000,000 kilowatts of electricity were produced, and in the mid-sixties more than a trillion kilowatts, an increase by 180 times in about sixty years. In the Soviet Union produc-

1. Encyclopaedia Britannica.

tion in the main industries has increased as follows (in 1,000 metric tons, electricity in million kilowatts):

	1913	1940	1960	1965	1970 (plan)
coal	29,100	165,900	513,600	578,000	670,000
crude petroleum	9,200	31,100	147,600	243,000	350,000
electricity	1,900	48,300	291,600	507,000	845,000
steel	4,200	18,300	65,280	91,200	126,500
cement	1,500	5,700	45,480	72,400	102,500

These are only the barest facts. However, they do make it clear that development of heavy industry has been far more rapid, both relatively and absolutely, in the United States than in the Soviet Union. Development of light industry and particularly of transport and agriculture was even more rapid in the United States. But there is no need to cite more figures. These industries are known to have developed more slowly in the Soviet Union and to lag behind heavy industry. The same sources reveal that Soviet development has been slower than development in Germany after the 1871 unification; and since the last war Soviet reconstruction has, by all accounts, been slower than reconstruction in Japan.[2] It is also important to point out that labor pro-

2. Japan is the fifth industrial state in the world, with five per cent of the world's industrial production. No Western country has had such rapid industrial growth since World War II. During the last thirty years industrial production in Japan has increased fivefold, and the country will soon be the third industrial power in the world. Its next five-year plan provides for a rise in production that

ductivity in the United States at the beginning of this century was one and a half times higher than in Western Europe, and four times higher than in the Soviet Union —Kosygin has admitted to its now being about twice as high—and to date the gap has not been closing, if it has not been actually widening, in spite of Communist stories of the absolute superiority of their system of ownership and the "abolition of exploitation" in their countries.

I am prepared to believe that scholars engaged in these matters are capable of finding many convincing explanations for the Soviet Union's lagging behind, while its peoples in a specific situation have been provided with superior benefits by the new Soviet regime. Yet no rational person of integrity can endorse the Soviet system's claims to a universal superiority, beyond time and space, simply on the grounds that it is "social-

---

will outstrip that of Germany and Great Britain by 1971. In the last three decades electrical energy has risen from 30 to 240 billion kilowatts, steel production from 6 to 51 million tons, and in two years' time it will have risen to 77 million tons. Japan takes first place for imports of iron ore, first for shipbuilding, with 47 per cent of the world's tonnage. The largest vessels are being built in Japanese yards, including giant tankers larger than 200,000 tons. Japan is also first in the production of radio receivers and transistors; and its telecommunications industry is among the most modern in the world. The country takes second place in the production of television sets, refrigerators, cotton fiber, synthetic rubber, and synthetic fibers, and third place in the production of steel, plastic materials, cement, sulphuric acid, wool fiber, cotton textiles, paper, and in the motor-vehicle industry. (*Politika,* Belgrade, April 7, 1968.)

ist," just as no power on earth can convince all nations of the peerlessness of the American way of life, in spite of the Americanization of the world in technology and production.

Theory is gray, while the tree of life is evergreen, said Goethe. As in the past, every nation must now find its own path. Today the world is dominated by two nuclear superpowers, the United States and the Soviet Union, while a third, China, which is beginning to tower, has a new role and significance because the possession of nuclear ballistic missiles could enable it to outterrorize all terrors. But the nuclear powers are the slaves of their own strength, because none of them possesses, nor in all probability ever will, a means of defense that would allow them to risk using the most destructive weapons. Warfare with conventional weapons against a resolute enemy, as the Vietnam war has shown, is too costly today and it is ineffectual. We live in a "nuclear peace, i.e., an industrial war." [3] This creates great difficulties, but also new opportunities for small and undeveloped countries: they need not submit unconditionally to the will of the great, highly developed countries, but neither can they survive and develop in isolation from the large economic and political communities.

That is the actual position of the small, undeveloped countries, and that is how it has always been, rather than as has been described by Simone de Beauvoir in *Les Belles Images:* "In all countries, whether socialist or

3. Quoted in Jean-Jacques Servan-Schreiber, *Le Défi Américain,* Paris, 1967, p. 291.

capitalist, man is being crushed by technology, alienated from his work, fettered, and stupefied. Instead of stretching out for an abundance which does not exist, and perhaps never will, people ought to content themselves with a minimum standard of living, as some of the very poor communities still do, in Sardinia and Greece, for instance, where technology has not penetrated nor money corrupted. There people know a harsh happiness, because certain values are preserved, values that are truly human values—dignity, brotherhood, generosity, which give life a unique flavor. If the creation of new needs continues, mirages will multiply. When did this decline start? On the day when priority was given to science instead of wisdom, to utility instead of beauty. With the Renaissance, with rationalism, capitalism, scientism. So far, so good; but what is to be done now? Make an attempt to revive wisdom and a sense of beauty inside us and around us. Only a moral revolution, not a social, political, or technical one, can lead man to the truth he has lost." [4] I do not know what Madame de Beauvoir's "minimum standard of living" is, but I suspect it is a little more than what she is idealizing in "some of the very poor communities." Life in Sardinia may look "harshly happy" to Parisian left- and right-wing intellectual cliques, but I know from my own Montenegro, in spite of the "values preserved" there, "values that are truly human," just what life has been like—a life of hunger, hatred, and death. . . .

What is the use of moralizations? Who is going to

4. Quoted in *ibid.,* pp. 274–275.

assess human needs, and with what means, and for what purpose? Man has entered an electronic age in which inventions and their applications, which have materialized solely with the support of a higher general standard of education, will become the most important factors in production, perhaps, indeed, in the entire life of nations. William Jovanovich points out that education, particularly technical education, is inevitably becoming the most important industry, the most productive industry—the basis for all production.[5] Property relations and political relations must be adapted to it—the sooner and less painfully, the better. In any case it is inevitable. In the West, this adaptation is somehow taking place through an increase in the role played by government and public ownership, brought about as much by the demands of modern industry as by social pressures. "Modern power is the skill of inventiveness, *i.e.,* of investigation, and the skill to get the invention into production, *i.e.,* technology. The sources that have to be mined are no longer in the earth nor numerous, nor are they in the machines. They are in the human brain. More accurately, in men's capacity for concentrated thought and creation."[6] In the East, however, the greatest opposition is being put up by a despotic form of government: there the government has become the property of a single group, the party bureaucracy, and it is the most valuable property of all, since it brings

5. *Now, Barrabas,* New York, 1964, pp. 42–43; see also, "America Revisited: Radicalism and Alienation," *America Now,* New York, 1969.
6. Servan-Schreiber, *op. cit.,* p. 295.

all kinds of privileges. One can assume that nations which fail to find the strength and skill to carry out the appropriate adaptations will be made subordinate and exploited, in spite of the generosity and best intentions of the developed countries.

IV

The slowest and least ready stage of my emancipation from Marxist philosophical dogmatics has been my rejection of Marx's historical materialism, which is to say, his thesis that the level of the productive forces determines the relationships of production, and the mode of production and political and intellectual life generally. The so-called socialist ownership under Communism was the greatest obstacle in the way of the maturation of my critical faculties and organized thinking, although, fairly early, while writing *The New Class,* and also, with still greater clarity, during my 1956–1961 imprisonment, I had felt that this was the *bête noire,* responsible both for the deep-rooted failures of Communism and for the interminable length of the paths leading out of its labyrinth. I found guidance in Marxian teaching and in my own revolutionary experience: from Marx I learned abstractly, and from the Yugoslav revolution and the social and party ferments of Yugoslavia today I had the experience to make me realize that ruling groups and forces resist change mainly from fear of losing economic privileges, fear that the system of ownership that allows them their material advantages (and often other advantages as well) will be destroyed. It is now quite clear to me that the problem is much more complex, but the breaches of Marx's idealist doctrine by insatiable Communist dignitaries, who had until recently been revolutionaries and proletarian leaders, were sufficient, at the beginning, to prompt my suspicions and compel me to think about things as they actually are. And when the Central Committee of the Yugoslav Communist League settled accounts with me in January of 1954, the real relationships and unidealistic interests erupted overnight in all their starkness: among the Central Committee members were people prepared to stone me in a fit of remorse for their own heresy, which had been "unmasked" and "proven" in me. More than that, there were some whose ideas and ideals had become so soft in their lives of power and comfort that they averted their eyes from me, as though I were some dead dog, although they would have gladly been on my side "if the chips had fallen differently," if, in short, somehow or other the balance of forces had come down in my favor. It was a bitter pill, but one that has to be swallowed once one has made up his mind to go through with an experience and learn from it. . . .

When the first sentence was passed on me by the party, I was not choked by the slime and poison of forlorn illusions. I did not accept falsehood for the truth, or treachery for necessity. Even today I am not capable of explaining why I acted as I did, but I maintain that courage, except insofar as it was identified with conscience, played a small part, and that the decisive factor was the realization that I was creating something new. The truths that had absorbed my transformed self and were relentlessly devouring it were something that I could not reject, even if I had wanted to. I had been aware, of course, ever since I could remember, that falsehood and coercion were inevitabilities of politics, and that may have been why I had never been able to bring myself to use them as weapons in the ideological struggle, particularly not the sort that cropped up among Communists. As in 1948, during Stalin's attacks on Yugoslavia, and his East European slander campaign against the Yugoslav leaders, so now my consciousness and conscience gave each other no respite, and drove me to seek an answer to these questions: What sort of government is it that finds its strength, and its justification before its own people, in falsehoods? What is the destination of a society that maintains and restores itself with injustice? What remains of ideas and ideals once they become means of terror and intimidation among their own adherents? What are the real aims and interests of people who have recourse to slander and coercion even toward those most in sympathy with their own views? Why are we Communists, once in power, more exclusive and unapproachable than anyone else? Why am I pilloried when my tormentors themselves know that I only wanted socialism to be closer to the people, in order to make socialism freer and more Yugoslav?

But at that time, in 1948, I was at odds with a world that was mine in idea, but that had no ties to the fabric of my being, my impulses, my way of life at the time; and so I found answers within the framework of the idea itself. And in 1954 and subsequently—after the Central Committee had passed sentence on me—I was in disagreement with my comrades about the job that we had done together. There was a split in my inner self—in my past, my way of life, my hopes. . . . Has not the same thing happened, in a different way, with others, with all the heretics, all those who have chosen their own vision rather than the existing realities of life? Recently did not a remarkable and thoroughly courageous woman, Svetlana Alliluyeva, daughter of Stalin, resurrect from satanic depths the conscience of her father, which had been sacrificed by him to an absolute faith, to the identification of his being with the hypothetical laws of history?

After the verdict on me had been delivered, mortal fear fanned out around me—the only living being to merge heart and soul with me was my second wife, Štefanija. Into a malign, dehumanized void was dissipated all that I had learned, all that I believed in. I buried myself in books, even those on nuclear physics and biology. I busied myself with sketching out literary ideas and jotting down reminiscences. But there were no answers or solutions outside myself, outside the harsh and unexpected reality.

And as I burned up my former self with my own thoughts and lifeblood, I was haunted by a remark Aneurin Bevan once made in a conversation with Vladimir Dedijer and me. His wife was with him, and we were all spending the night at a country cottage near Pljevlja, sometime in the summer of 1953. As far as I can remember, the conversation was on the subject of the way in which the future socialism and traditional political freedoms were being married in Britain. I pointed out, and Bevan did not demur, that in Yugoslavia it could take the form of workers' self-management, and he exclaimed, "A mixed economy." Bevan's formulation applied to Great Britain: he maintained that it was necessary only to nationalize industry that would be efficient, or more efficient, if nationalized, while other industries would remain in private or cooperative hands. In Yugoslavia, and more particularly in the other East European countries, this formulation does not seem to me to be workable, even today. There the middle class has almost been destroyed, and even the small business concerns have been nationalized. Nevertheless, in Bevan's thinking there was something in common with what I came to recognize later, which is that the sterility of Communism, and its limitedness, the impossibility of carrying out any reforms, actually spring from the system of ownership. Ownership in Communism is social or national in form and, as such, contrived and made absolute, while the actual management and control is in the hands of party bureaucrats working through departments of state and the economy.

All this was known to me by the time I had completed *The New Class* in 1956, and I pondered its deeper significance during my term of imprisonment. Although "socialist ownership" was no longer sacrosanct to me, I was still unable to find a clear, unambiguous alternative to it—ways and means by which it could be replaced. This was out of the question until a few years' development in Yugoslavia would provide sufficient facts to work on, and until, on my release from prison on December 31, 1966, I could gain a more comprehensive picture of the real situation—the state of the economy, the problems and dilemmas of people's lives.

At the time of my second release from prison, Yugoslavia was in the throes of its so-called economic reform, a reform to which Yugoslav policy had been driven too late and out of harsh necessity, with the pressure of deficits and economic backwardness as the decisive factors rather than an analytical and undoctrinaire appreciation of conditions and methods necessary to a modern economy. All the officials, of course, were talking about the reform. Its objectives, which were geared to the present condition and future targets of the economy, were not bad in themselves—profitability, a link with the world market, the free movement of goods and capital, currency convertibility, and managerial efficiency and economies in the administration. But in practice people were putting no effort into making a success of the reform, and they could not do so because the old political and administrative structure was still there and the ownership structure was unchanged, *i.e.*, the same monopoly of party bureaucracy was guardian and controller. In agriculture, state properties, largely uneconomic, were still in the foreground, while millions of peasants remained exposed to the depredations of bureaucratic and monopolistic co-operatives and to the arbitrariness of local officials. In the same way, the craft industries, the catering or service industries, and small trading remained in a state of stagnation, while the so-called "socialist sector" was, more often than not, incapable of meeting increased needs. And, most important of all, there was an inflexibility in the so-called "state property." Industry, banking, transport, energy, and the greater part of commerce were bound by the party bureaucracy's power monopoly, which was all the more unbearable because it was still, to a large extent, *also a decision-making monopoly in the economy.* Unwillingly at first, and in a disorganized manner, but later as an emergency and out of sheer necessity, Yugoslavia became a substantial exporter of labor, and an exporter—to make the irony complete—to West European countries, for foreign capitalist exploitation. The import of foreign capital was announced and the necessary legislation passed. But this has not taken place on any major scale, because under the legal conditions, to say nothing of the economic and political conditions, which were all laid down by the guardians of the working people, the watchdogs of socialism, foreign capital is not greatly encouraged. Things like this, obsolete features and recipes, are too constricting for any economy, let alone for a modern socialist one. . . . I anticipated this in *The New Class,* in the chapter called "The Ideological Economy" (a title that appeared in translation as "Dogmatism in the Economy"). This is now taken for granted in Yugoslavia, and in one way or another it will be, sooner or later, throughout Eastern Europe.

So much, then, for any marriage between my ideas about the roots of Communist despotism and Bevan's reflections on freedom under British socialism. A mixed economy in Yugoslavia, which is now a fact and has always been latent, can never, even in the future, be similar, let alone identical, to Britain's mixed economy. Because in Britain, according to Bevan, what was happening was that private enterprise was gradually being nationalized in sectors where this makes for greater efficiency, all without weakening the British parliamentary system, while in Yugoslavia the problem is to achieve political freedoms and the liberation of huge nationalized industries and private concerns from the managerial grip of a self-perpetuated party bureaucracy.

But human destinies are strange and unpredictable. Bevan was a product of the harshness of the Welsh mines, of industrialism and the British parliamentary system, while I grew out of the privations of Montenegro, out of intellectual unrest and the irresistible drive of a somewhat primitive society toward an industrial state. Nevertheless, our thoughts grew together, and a friendship developed between us. And that is why dogma-straitened and dried-up minds accuse me of having come under the influence of the British Labourites, Bevan in particular. In that respect Bevan had a more fortunate destiny; if anyone had entertained the notion that by associating with Yugoslav Communists he might have picked up some of their ideas, that would not have done any harm to his reputation. Bevan remained steadfast in his demands for my release. His death in 1960 was a deep shock to me, but it did not affect my thinking. If any of the ideas of that clever and courageous man have entered my thinking, it is just another proof of the impossibility of isolated systems these days. Genuine ideas never have been isolated.

V

Although some of the substance of Communism is still active in all Communist countries—chiefly the one-party system and the party bureaucracy monopoly over the economy—the international relations and international position of each country differ so radically today from any other that to treat them all as the same would be the gravest conceivable mistake. That is why some of the views I expressed in *The New Class* about national Communism, and the possibility of a change in Communism generally, need to be developed further today.

This is what I particularly have in mind: one, the assumption that every Communist state born of revolution necessarily develops into a national government, or, rather, into a form of national Communism; two, the assumption that Communism is in a state of flux, though remaining unchanged in essence—a monopoly of power over the economy and the life of the nation as a whole.

The differences and conflicts between the Soviet Union and Albania, between the Soviet Union and China, and between China and Cuba and the Soviet

Union have, in fact, confirmed my first assumption. Further, relations between Communist governments and between Communist parties have now reached a state where this assumption can be held to apply to all Communist governments and parties everywhere, namely, that every Communist government, as soon as it achieves stability, strives to stand on its own feet and to subordinate all its objectives to national ideals and opportunities, while every Communist party, even if not in power, strives for political independence from the Communist great powers. In other words, just as peoples and nations in the past have survived in the shadow of various social movements and formations, so they survive in the shadow of Communism today, compelling the Communists to adapt to their ethos, aspirations, and potentialities. The shortcomings of my second assumption, however, are owing not only to the change in the actual situation, but also to my philosophical outlook at the time, with its roots in Aristotle and Marx, an outlook in which it is possible, at least in interpretation, to separate form from substance. Moreover, from the footnotes in *The New Class* it can be inferred that, at the time, I maintained that changes of substance (in that particular case, social changes) take place solely through an inner destruction, not by their gradual transformation. That particular assumption has to be modified today with the statement that Communism is changing in its own essence, but without making the corollary that it has already changed, let alone specifying a mode of change valid for all countries. Quite the reverse: out of the tendency for Communist movements to turn into national movements, the human mind inevitably draws the conclusion (though in real life nothing takes place according to the rules of logic) that the transformation of Communist movements will take place in a manner peculiar to each country.

The analyses and inferences of *The New Class* are, for the most part, based on what I know about Soviet and Yugoslav Communism and about the conflict between them. This is understandable, since Communism was then at the beginning of its national and internal social regrouping. Today, however, no Communist government, or group of governments and parties, is able to make use of sufficient and trustworthy generalizations. And while I pointed out in *The New Class* that Communism, precisely because it is in a state of flux, should be subjected to a thorough investigation at every stage of its development, today I have to add: every attempt to make a generalization for Communism leads to errors and a general fiasco. The road to understanding and recovery can be found only by scrutinizing Communism in each country separately, and each, also, discretely within the Communist superpowers' spheres of influence. In reality, Communism no longer exists. Only national Communisms exist, each different in doctrine and in the policies practiced and in the actual state of affairs they have created. What binds the Communists together today in international relations, or makes them want to be bound together, is fear of perils at home and abroad, or is the result of pressures from one of the Communist superpowers. Only nominally do Communists exhibit a mournful nostalgia for the imaginary "paradise lost" of world brotherhood. And as far as Soviet and Yugoslav Communism is concerned, even though their once-bitter quarrel has come down to the level of doctrinaire pontifications and diplomatic maneuverings, their mutual differences are exceedingly great today. This is their relative position: Soviet Communism has become the mainstay of conservative Communist forces at home and abroad, while Yugoslav Communism is a model of the weakness and disintegration of Communism, both in theory and practice, and at the same time is a model for national Communism and a hope for democratic transformation.

The problems of Communism, and of people living under Communism, are in their very nature wider and more complex than any human mind could embrace or unravel. But some features of Communism, some of its characteristics, have, with time, become clear and unequivocal within a given political and social context. On examining these features, one's mind conceives of certain metaphors: it is as if the creator were scorning his own handiwork; or as if the handiwork were bearing witness with its dying, failing hand to the teaching of its creator. Under Communism the productive forces have come into conflict with the relationships of production; and if we substitute "party" for "capital," then we can see before our eyes a vision of Communism's destiny, the one Marx had assigned to capitalism: "Monopoly capital [party monopoly] becomes fetters on the mode of production which flourished with it and under it." [1]

We can now perceive that the revolt against the Com-

1. *Capital,* Vol. I, p. 645.

munists' power monopoly and monopolistic designs on the management and control of the economy has come from those very forms for life that the Communists believed would, with the necessary encouragement, be reliable. This holds true both for the so-called socialist or social ownership which prevails in Yugoslavia and which in the other socialist countries amounts to nearly the whole of the national wealth, and also for the government itself, and even the party itself.

This property, *i.e.*, the national economy, consisting of structures fossilized by monopoly and dogma, has reached so low a point in its development and in its international and political relations that it is no longer in a position to recuperate, let alone to cope with unanticipated competition from Western economies equipped with more modern techniques and regulated more and more by electronic devices. To put the matter simply, Communism has in the main shown itself capable of effecting the transformation of a craft and peasant economy, albeit with harsh and costly methods; but it has plunged into difficulties, as was inevitable, because it now has to pass out of the industrial stage, with the aid of electronics and massive education programs and the employment of skilled scientific workers, into a new and more complex stage—the age of automation and mass production and mass consumption.

The same problems, in another form, have already appeared, and will continue to do so, in the developed Western countries: monopolies had to be prohibited, or at least kept within bounds; private enterprise in various forms has been supplemented in various ways by state and co-operative enterprise; and the role of the state as co-ordinator and planner has everywhere been considerably strengthened. This does not mean that private property has been abolished in the West; and it could hardly be said to have been curbed. It is simply no longer the exclusive form of ownership. The standard of living, the inexorable drive of the Western nations toward new, more modern methods of production and toward complete accommodation to scientific achievements—these factors have been making the structure of ownership more mobile and diversified. This means that all the sacred cows have been killed or hamstrung—except those in the minds of men. These changes and accommodations started a long time ago, with the joint-stock companies, like everything human, stumbling into troubles (monopolies), becoming faced with stoppages (crises), which the people had to control or eliminate by the exercise of strife and ingenuity. . . . But the Communists have forgotten, or prefer not to admit, that none other than Marx himself had this to say, in *Capital:* "The capitalist joint-stock companies should be considered, just as the co-operative factories, as forms in transition from the capitalist to the collective mode of production, except that in the former antagonism is abolished negatively, while in the latter it is abolished positively."

Something similar, but in a forced and roundabout way, is happening with the so-called socialist property in Yugoslavia, and also in other East European countries, although in a different and more concealed form —even in the Soviet Union, Bulgaria, and Eastern Germany, in spite of the stability of the bureaucracy in the

Soviet Union, the servile obedience of the top leadership in Bulgaria, and the doctrinaire brutality in Eastern Germany. Government debts and the lack of funds to meet foreign payments have now forced the Yugoslav authorities to slacken the reins on the "small" (private) service industries and catering concerns. Unemployment is compelling them to do the same with the private craftsmen, and the chronic shortage of capital has roused the slumbering "socialist" economists not only to recommend the entry of foreign capital, but also to discuss the issue of shares by socialist firms for sale to the public.

This does not mean that there is a crisis in Yugoslavia, or anywhere else, of social, or socialist, ownership, or that it is doomed. What is in crisis and disintegration is the privileged position of the Communists over various types of publicly owned property, and their prerogatives in certain departments of state, without which they would no longer be the power in society that they are. The elimination of this Communist monopoly would mean that public property and the authority of the state would constitute truly *national* ownership as well as freedom.

No one can tell in advance what will be the fate of any particular pattern of public ownership taken as a whole once it is given free play, because today, as a result of the reckless greed among the Communists, some aspects have been extended to industries or areas where not only was there no need for nationalization in the interests of the nation or society, but also where it has actually resulted in a decline in the quality of goods produced, and even in quantity. Examples of this are the craft industries, some of the most important sectors of agriculture, and the greater part of the service industries. As is known, it is not only technical factors that play their part in changing the patterns of ownership, but also human passions and organized social forces. Once publicly owned property has been emancipated from the tutelage of party and other bureaucracies, I do not see any rational reason for making any changes (or any power that could do this) except those required to shape it in the way intended by the men who created it with their sweat and brains, *i.e.*, as property that is socialist through and through, and national, really so, not merely a demagogic cliché born of dogma and self-delusion. I stress this not as a partisan of democratic socialism, or yet as a politician seeking workable solutions for his own country. The development of ownership patterns in Western countries shows that the socialist or national form of ownership, provided it is free from the domination of political and other bureaucratic monopoly, and is not the only form of ownership, an absolute one, is a suitable way of applying modern techniques that broaden the horizons of modern life as well as reduce social inequalities. . . . Although the only value of analogies is that they can make us examine, a comparison between Communism and feudalism is not out of place here. First of all, in a Communist system the top leaders of the oligarchy distribute state functions, and sometimes economic functions, among party officials, just like the fiefs which the kings and barons used to grant to their faithful and deserving vassals; secondly, there is the parasitism of both feudalism and Communism with the development of a market and industrial economy. On this latter point, it seems that in the same way that the royal prerogative, the privileges of the feudal lords, and the feudal estates, became a stumbling block to free trade and industry, which were developing under feudalism, so the despotism of the oligarchy, and the party bureaucracy's privileges in the government and the economy, together with the static, absolutized property patterns providing a basis for all this, have put the brakes on modern transport, modern management, and modern technology, and even on the socially owned property that has developed under Communism.

The emancipation of national property under Communism cannot take place without changes in political and social relationships; once change has been achieved, it will bring about further changes—both in social and in property relationships. In Yugoslavia it was shown that when, due to the need to change to a market economy, the role of the party and other bureaucracies was weakened in nationalized industry, the result was a weakening in "socialist" property as well, but only in those areas where nationalization had been forced through by ideological prejudice and the parasitic needs of the political bureaucracy, where it was not, in fact, socialist. The kolkhozes (collective farms) have been dissolved, and private peasant holdings established; private enterprise in the service industries has been revived; forms of so-called joint-owned enterprise have appeared, and so on. The inevitable conclusion is that Communist systems are moving toward a diversified pattern of ownership. Even socialist property, free at last of political parasites and bureaucratic managers, will have to change, augmenting its management structures and methods and adapting them to meet the demands of modern technology and the world market. . . . But when it comes to justifying the establishment and development of private enterprise, something which economic necessity is already imposing to some extent in certain fields in Yugoslavia, there is no cause to suppose that the Communists will fail to find good "socialist" and "Marxist" theories in their inexhaustible arsenal of dogmatism, provided that the new owners do not threaten the Communists' property monopoly of government. . . .

All reorganizations and reforms under Communism hitherto have only changed the method of establishing "the leading role of the party," which is to say, the form of the party bureaucracy's privileges. Now, at least as far as Yugoslavia is concerned—and what was sought, and now frustrated, in Czechoslovakia, too—industrial and social relations have reached a stage where further development is impossible without substantial changes. These changes are moves toward greater freedom of operation for existing patterns of ownership and greater freedom in setting up new ones; in other words, in the direction of abolition of the single political group monopoly, even of the single party line dominating society and the economy. Because the Yugoslav economy today is suffering from repeated disruptions, unemployment, inconsistent production as well as overproduction, shortage of capital, and heavy debts—all those troubles that the Marxists have shown to be "exclusive" and "incurable" ailments of capitalism (and from which capitalism has indeed itself suffered). Even had the Czechs and

Slovaks wrested freedoms boldly and skillfully from the hands of Stalinist despotism at home and abroad, I think that numerous difficulties would still have been in store for them, difficulties that would be all the greater because of the high level of their economy and the presumably high degree of their independence from their Soviet "elder brother." But even in momentary defeat they can take comfort in the knowledge that in other Communist countries, and even in the Soviet Union, forces are at work, the forces of change and greater social freedom.

The future is known only to the gods and to dogmatists. But even we mortals can see that the Communists have fallen into two "mortal errors": first, the prescription they wrote out for the Western systems has not worked, because Western systems have refused to die, and, instead, have carried on their technological progress; second, life in the Communist countries has dared to go beyond the bounds they laid down for it. The property structure the Communists established, idealizing it because their existence and privileges depend upon it, is not, in its present state of subordination to the monopoly of party management and control, capable of adapting itself to the realities of the outside world or of fulfilling its own potentialities—to make secure provision for the life of the nation. Up to the present no nation has been prepared to lay down its life for the beauty of a dogma; and no nation is going to find Communist dogma the exception. Yugoslavia today is an example of the collapse of Communist illusions, but it is also—alongside Czechoslovakia, of course—an example of the beginning of new patterns inside the old; the leaven of discontent is working inside the so-called socialist property structure itself and among the disgruntled and betrayed, but undiscouraged, Communists. Communist privileges in government and the economy are today the only social obstacle, the only real obstacle in the way of Yugoslavia's fervent and spontaneous hopes, and indeed those of the whole of Eastern Europe, that their economies would be integrated with the economy of Europe—and that amounts to demands by the people in all these countries for freedom.

A united Europe was until quite recently also one of my ideals. And although Yugoslavia's entry in the European Common Market is still, to my mind, a vital necessity for the life of the country, I am no longer so convinced that a united Europe is capable of being a separate power in the world, if indeed it needs to play that role at all. And such a possibility seems all the less likely, since these days the meaning of Europe is rarely taken to include Russia, although up to the present the fate of the two has been inseparable. De Gaulle expressed this, with his slogan "Europe from the Atlantic to the Urals." Europe today, with leadership in many fields of knowledge lost and some of its technology outstripped, is too small and too poor without Russia to be matched *en bloc* against new powers, the United States, China, Japan, and, of course, Russia itself. What De Gaulle did not realize, or was unwilling to realize, is that Russia, by virtue of its internal system and hegemonic claims, is in opposition to Europe. It is still to be hoped that the Chinese threat abroad and the unprofitability of Russia's isolated internal development and the long-range impracticability of its hegemonic designs will lead to a merger between Russia and Europe. This will be the more likely because the freer structures here discussed are essential for providing a further boost to the Russian people, whose immeasurable sufferings and unsparing sacrifices were the only force capable of swamping the two modern despotisms that subjugated Europe and threatened the whole world: Napoleon's dictatorship of reason and Hitler's dictatorship of unreason. . . . I often dream and play with the thought that Khrushchev was only the harbinger of great reforms and that the great reformer has yet to come—someone more like Alexander II than Peter I, because today the problem is one of expanding and guaranteeing human potentialities and values rather than national ones. . . . But hopes do not make history, nor has anyone caught up with time past: the East European countries, Yugoslavia certainly, cannot wait for such a state of affairs in Europe and Russia, even if they could bet on a certainty. They already have to link their economies with the West European economy and to free their economic and human forces for these wider, more complex conditions. Europe, it seems, can survive without association with these countries, in the same way that in the nineteenth century it was no crucial matter to Europe whether Serbia and Rumania were independent and whether Poland remained divided. But these countries cannot survive without Europe. Neither, it is true, can they survive without the United States and the Soviet Union, or, indeed, without Asia—because world history's center of gravity has shifted west and east of Europe. Europe is the area that makes these countries a part of the world, and is an essential aspect of their economic and cultural viability.

VI

May Marx forgive me one last dereliction: the crisis in Communism is not brought about by economic, so-called objective factors, but almost exclusively by human, so-called subjective factors. Strangely enough, these subjective factors are not ideas that grip the masses and so lead to material power. Rather, they are individual acts, a human defiance of coercion, whether that coercion takes the form of brute force or of spiritual domination or, as is most frequently the case, of a mixture of the two. The unfortunate human race, the wretched human being, will endure all evils, even coercion, for as long as it can and must; it will never submit to them.

Long ago Aristotle discovered that every human community is a community of diverse aspirations. This confirms that no system ever can be good for, and acceptable to, all men. No objection can be made even to Communism on the score that it is no better than other systems, although that it is happens to be precisely its own illusion. Similarly, the collapse of despotisms is never caused by the degree of their harshness; the collapse comes when human consciousness is ready to accept that the despotism is absurd and irrational, *i.e.,* no longer capable of justifying its existence as a satisfaction of human needs.

Because of this, the intellectually fastidious person, as well as the man in the street (if such a person exists), puts up with Communism in spite of its seeming to be "unnatural" to him. At the same time, for its part, Communism, however brutally, does resolve vital problems of some nations which other social systems, for one reason or another, have been incapable of doing.

From its very inception as an idea, Communism has been accompanied by doubts as to its practicability; from the first moment of its establishment, there has been, within its own ranks, discontent over a gulf between its promises and its practices. The reason is that Communism, like every other revolutionary despotism, has failed to bring itself into harmony, let alone identify itself, with unidealized, natural desires, and with the ordinary everyday life of the people. Sooner or later a "more natural" unidealized system has to be substituted for Communism's violent revolutionary role. This is not to say that the revolutionary role is eccentric—it is a role for which certain societies and nations in our time have had a need, as have other societies and nations at other times, each with a different pattern of violent revolutionary movements and coups. There is an inevitability imposed by the very nature and historical role of every revolutionary doctrine and every revolution. A way of life without any determinable ultimate objective but that of keeping alive will eventually abandon Communism as a revolutionary doctrine and form of government, having no regard for Communism's idealistic objectives and still less for the good intentions and qualities of its leaders.

The economic and social relationships introduced by Communism, although they are a hotbed of new ideas and prototypes, are not in themselves the cause of its conflict with the currents of life. There may be no cause at all, at least not in a single and unmistakable form. It may simply be that with time a store of knowledge is accumulated and social circumstances are shifted, so that even the Communists themselves no longer believe in Communism, while in ordinary workaday life there persist abominable stereotypes—the imprints of Marxist ideology, as it were—that provide the leaders of Communist society with their pattern of reference. Today the most egregious and deep-rooted failures of Communism are neither the result of resistance by the "class enemy," since he hardly exists any longer, nor the result of the aggressive intentions of the "imperialists," since the Communists accept "imperialists" as equal partners in the era of "nuclear holocaust" or, at the least, manage to live in peace and co-operation with them.

The failures spring from inside Communism itself, which is why, it would seem, they become the harder to reverse the more that Communism is left to its own resources. Communism is hard pressed by the very forces of life. Its gravediggers are its own more or less doctrinaire pragmatists; in one generation the same leaders turn from revolutionaries into despots, and then from despots into "liberals" who use Communist ideas as a coinage for settling their bills. The Communist leaders' frequent changes of doctrinal clothing, together with their stupid resistance to superficial life styles, no less than their deluded resistance to the facts of life, make Communism —once the hope and the beacon for millions of fighters who sacrificed everything for it—ugly in its disintegration, uglier than any other outdated system in the past. In betokening reality, the poets already sense that Communism is about to decimate its sacred cows.

The playwright and satirist Matija Bećković, using a pseudonym, wrote of Yugoslav society in 1967 in this vein: "In 1945, many of today's ordinary everyday occurrences would have been unlikely, inconceivable. At that time no one could possibly have believed that within twenty years tens of thousands of Yugoslavs would be working abroad. Only reactionaries could possibly have believed that Communist partisans, the war veterans of Yugoslavia, would in some cases be working under the direction of German war veterans. No one ever imagined that students would go on working as milk deliverymen, or that the children of revolutionaries would have separate schooling. Arguments like these had been very effective in compromising the *bourgeoisie*. Who was to know at that time that there would be progressive monarchs in the world, and that we should be on friendly terms with many of them? Not even people with the most idiosyncratic imaginations, for whom nothing is sacred, ever dreamed that the Nazi war criminal Erih Rajakovič would come to Yugoslavia with his family for a holiday. Few people knew that churches and palaces were part of our cultural heritage, a priceless historical treasure. There were people who had returned from the future to give their impressions to the nation. They maintained, and people believed them, that there would be none of these things: prostitutes, night clubs, gambling casinos, strip-tease clubs, corruption, financial disparities, wages or salaries, civil servants, domestic help, fashions, mistresses and servants, or even road sweepers.

"Only the most incorrigible could possibly have believed that we should close schools in mourning for American presidents, smoke American cigarettes, drink American liquor, chew American gum, wear Italian shoes, drink Spanish wine, eagerly buy German cars, sing cowboy songs. . . .

"Who would have believed that German war veterans would marry our daughters and sisters and would become welcome and valued tourists?

"All these things are commonplace today. It was inevitable. At one time there has been one lot of fallacies to come to terms with, at another time there has been another. The impossible has become the probable. . . ." [1]

That kind of irony constitutes a piece from the jigsaw of Yugoslavia today, where the disintegration and transformation of Communism seems to be more multifarious and conspicuous than in any other East European country or in Communism as a world movement. There are differences, of course, because of different conditions and different openings available to the party bureaucracies—in other words, "different roads to socialism" that can be taken by separate countries. All Communist par-

1. Dr. Janez Pacuk, "The Cinema as a Refrigerator for Illusions," *Svet*, Belgrade, Nov. 11, 1967, No. 577, p. 20.

ties and systems are now caught at the same time in the decline of the classical revolutionary pattern and in the birth of a new peacetime one. In Yugoslavia this manifests itself in the form of an economic crisis that may be insuperable, as well as in an ideational withering away of the party; in Poland, in the form of a conflict between the hard-core, doctrinaire pro-Soviet bureaucrats and the nationalist, democratic intellectuals in the party; in Czechoslovakia, in the form of a showdown that the freedom-seeking people, led by democratic Communists, are having with the remnants of Stalinism; in Rumania, in the form of nationalist resistance by both the top party leaders and the people to Soviet hegemony—and so on. In international Communism, "separatism" is taking place in the form of a deepening conflict between the two Communist superpowers, the Soviet Union and China, and a further estrangement of other Communist parties from both of them.

Thus the circle of interparty and intergovernment contradictions is closed: first the Soviet Union and then China, since they could not help being great powers, were forced to exert their hegemony over the weaker and unprotected Communist parties, and these were precisely the parties that defected, one after the other, for the sake of their own survival. Every state, every social group, for that matter, always has a natural desire for the status of equality. With the establishment of more and more Communist regimes, the time was bound to come when the once-accepted world center could no longer command unquestioning obedience, when it would become enfeebled, and when internationalism would end in formal dissolution. There, quickening in the womb of national frameworks, were the embryos of the heresies.

This historical development is, incidentally, further evidence that Communism is not a religion but a political movement, or, rather, a political authority of a special type: wherever it was first and foremost an ideology and thus endowed with many of the characteristics of a religion, it was possible, indeed essential, for it to have a definite center, but as soon as it became transformed into a number of different states, the process of dissolution was bound to take place. This invites comparisons. The origins of the schism in the Catholic church at the beginning of the sixteenth century lay in the opposition to papal secular authority by increasingly powerful princes, rather than in differing interpretations of dogma. But Catholicism purged itself as a religion in the Counter Reformation, and the gradual weakening of the Vatican's secular power resulted in an actual strengthening of its role as a religious world center. For the same reasons, if a logical forecast of history does not go awry, Communism is not threatened by internecine wars similar to those between Catholics and Protestants in the seventeenth century. Yet, because of the impending circumstances both inside and outside Communist countries, it is not out of the question that there may be all kinds of conflicts, even wars, between Communist countries—and these could become part of a wider area of conflict, on a world scale, if not the actual cause of such a conflict.

So the national and international differences and dissensions in the Communist world reflect and complement each other, with a steady tendency toward national emancipation and ideological diversity—in other words, toward the diminution of dogmatism. Disintegration or change in Communism is both a vertical and a horizontal process: vertical in that it is taking place in the Communist idea itself, in the movement on a world scale and in each party separately; and horizontal in that it is undergoing a steady multilateral breakaway, with the national parties separating from each other as well as from the Communist superpowers.

These upheavals in Communism are accompanied, and partly conditioned, by the restratification taking place in society itself and by the change in the balance of its forces. Thus, in the whole of the East European Communist world, in each East European country in a different guise and with varying intensity, *ground has already been covered for the creation of a new social stratum*—a special middle class recruited from all present-day strata, from the top of the party oligarchy itself to skilled workers and well-to-do peasants. The sum and substance of this new stratum of society are *specialists* of all kinds— artists, engineers, teachers, technicians, managers, and skilled political people. The new stratum is forming an undoctrinaire, even antidoctrinaire, class that is bent on raising its standard of living and keen on advancing technical capability and profitable business. It came into being spontaneously as a result of industrialization, and it grew from the environment and social relationships that industrial technology creates. As yet this social group, this emerging class, has thus far no ideology of its own, no or-

ganized pattern, although suggestions of both are beginning to show, even among its Communist members.
Among its members, more and more, are to be found in-
dependent-thinking theoreticians and democratic sym-
pathizers. The party bureaucracy has been unable to
check the emergence of this class because its members
are indispensable to the bureaucracy's own survival. The
bureaucracy cannot maintain power without the material advances provided by the industrial and cultural
transformation that the members of this class alone
can carry out. Moreover, the bureaucracy has been
forced to accord recognition and to make concessions
to members of this class and to prospective members
of it. Today, now that these people are established in
their own right as a force in society, all that the bureaucracy can do is chide them for their "deficiencies" in social awareness or for their "unsocialist" ethics, or make
them a target of political campaigns and administrative
trickery to curb their efforts to organize themselves. The
very fact that the growing strength of this class cannot
now be restrained—and that the growth of its privileges
in society will result in better living standards for the
rest of the nation as well—means that this is the class of
the future. . . . And although I do not expect this class
to improve immediately the freedoms of choice to any
great extent, I feel that I am in a sense its spokesman,
because I can at least envisage the inevitability of its
progress. . . . In my view, man's nature cannot be divorced today from the actual historical frame it occupies,
and the destiny of nations is expressed within that
frame. . . .

Because this sort of development has gone farthest in Yugoslavia, and because Yugoslavia is a multinational state, it is undoubtedly an excellent example of the vertical and horizontal disintegration of Communism and the restratification of society. Yugoslavia is also a living proof of Communism's unsuitability for contemporary life, an unsuitability that has a regular pattern everywhere, and of which Yugoslavia displays certain aspects —ideological, nationalistic, social. Sometimes one aspect is more in evidence, at other times another, but never is any divorced from the whole.

VII

What is actually happening in Yugoslavia?

The conflict between the Yugoslav revolution and Soviet great-power hegemony inevitably has had an influence on developments inside the country.

At the beginning, Yugoslavia's leaders resisted Soviet pressures by refuting the false accusations made against them and by competing with the Soviet party in revolutionary gymnastics. But experience soon showed that this sort of policy could at best only lead to a fine, heroic death, for it was cutting them off from the outside world and aggravating the confusion in their own ranks. In an hour of deadly peril for himself, Tito consented to an intensification of the ideological conflict with the Soviet leadership, and he also agreed to allow the first, albeit modest, liberalization measures—decentralization of management in the economy and decentralization of the state administration except for the political organs, the party, the secret police, and the army. In due course there were all kinds of changes. The Yugoslav state managed to stand on its own feet; the Yugoslav economy was harnessed to the market at home and abroad and lightened its administrative load, and the representatives of ideological unity in the party were compelled to make use of democratic demagogy.

Obviously all this did not proceed as simply as my brief description here suggests. Alongside the more liberal currents, the powerful revolutionary forces kept their course, having now been transformed into a backward-looking bureaucracy. One example of this was the collectivization of the countryside that was being carried out side by side with the liberalization of intellectual life and education. (This collectivization was not relinquished until the end of the first period of liberalization.) In other respects, too, the struggle against Stalin, although it had ushered in the disintegration of world Communism and helped to cause changes inside Communism, had its adverse consequences: with its idyllic picture of revolutionary brotherhood still undimmed (although it had never known a democratic flowering) the party was a breeding ground for the secret police, with all their usual authoritarian paraphernalia. Efforts to introduce a democratic spirit into the party, in order to give a boost to the liberalization of society and the economy, were opposed by the party's bureaucratic forces, which up to then had been holding the reins of power. Soon after Stalin's death, accounts were settled with the "revisionists" whose criticisms had been defiling and ravaging the party's "ideological unity," i.e., the ideological monopoly of the party oligarchy.

Hemingway wrote that revolutionary fervor can only be sustained by tyranny. The history of all dogmas, including that of Communism, as can be seen unmistakably in Yugoslavia today, testifies that a faith, once it has been contaminated by new truths, can never be restored; nor can the sacred unity of a church or a movement be re-established once it has been ravaged by the elimination of its most faithful believers. When the wheels of history turn back, they are never the same wheels; nor is it the same road along which they roll.

The intellectual undercurrents, the modifications in the economy, and the regroupings in society have slowly but surely done their work. Yugoslavia's ruling party, the Communist party, is no longer either a Stalinist or a Leninist party. The reason that the party still harks back nominally to Communism is to be found both in its origins and in the insatiable need felt by the manipulators of Communist ideology for self-deception.

The differentiation between a "Leninist" and a "Stalinist" party may seem purely a matter of dogmatics, but it is important. Stalin not only insisted on "ideational unity"—in other words, the monolithic party—but actually he achieved it, by the most brutal methods. On the other hand, Lenin permitted (though admittedly in an erratic and limited fashion) a variety of opinions in the party to be publicly aired. Party leaders today, when glorying in the "return to Leninist party rules," are chasing a chimera, because these "rules" are now reduced to a more punctilious observance of the statutory regulations rather than applied in the original Leninist sense—guaranteed rights for the party minority, majority voting in the party on the basis of different points of view and different policies. No Communist party in power, not even the Yugoslav Communist League, has ever adopted these genuinely Leninist rules. (Significantly, the new draft statute of the Czechoslovak Communist party makes provision for these rules.)

Relationships within Communist parties, and in societies ruled by Communist parties, are only ostensibly going in this direction; the return to Lenin and his party "rules," like the return to the young Marx and his doctrine of alienation, is no more than the usual Communist flight into mythology, and in this instance a spectral and anachronistic mythology.

In spite of the resistance at the top, and in spite of official declarations, the evolution of the Communist parties is in fact leading to the disintegration of their ideology and to their own metamorphosis into increasingly heterogeneous trends, often in conflict, however ideologically similar. One can predict that soon Communist leaders will devise makeshift measures for camouflage purposes, and launch back-to-Lenin-and-Marx campaigns. Yet the whole drift in Eastern Europe is sweeping toward the weakening of doctrinaire and the strengthening of freer and more vital approaches to contemporary conditions.

The present situation in all East European countries, and particularly in Czechoslovakia and Yugoslavia, shows that the Communist leaders have been compelled to adopt new, freer courses in order to avoid isolation from the outside world—to avoid the dangers that lie in the fact of their countries' backwardness. At first, however, these new courses primarily affected the practice of the arts and the development of the economy; yet they inevitably led to an undermining of the party's monolithic uniformity and to its destratification. I do not wish to imply that all Communists everywhere are always against modern art. I am merely making the point that the new art forms are necessarily bound to unadaptable, self-contained modes of thinking. In the same way, a market economy is unfeasible in the presence of any sort of monopoly; political monopoly introduces into economic life and conditions certain antieconomic forces, and it loads the economy with inessential, arbitrary burdens.

The worst trouble in Yugoslavia, and in Czechoslovakia, too, arose from failure to realize these truths before it was too late, if they have yet been realized at all. A return to ideological unity in the party and to an ideologically administered economy, which Yugoslavia attempted between 1962 and 1966, is impossible without arousing opposition and causing incalculable confusion and waste. It should be stressed that the slowdowns and disruptions in the Yugoslav economy, which have been a drag everywhere in the life of the country for the past several years, are not the result, as Stalinist and other dogmatists maintain, of failure to apply good Marxist theory correctly, nor are they, as official and semiofficial reformers claim, the result of unsuitable and obsolete administration, for similar troubles are apparent in all the East European countries.

In Yugoslavia it was inevitable that a conflict would come, as it already has, between the economy and the official policy, that there would occur a polarization within society. On one side are the intellectual and educationally creative forces outside and inside the party, backed by the new social group of technicians and business managers, and, potentially, by the general public; while on the other side there is the decreasing number of the political bureaucrats, the designers of the so-called "political factories" (*i.e.,* factories built for political and doctrinaire reasons rather than for economic needs), the rural bureaucrats, and the technically backward political appointees in industry. But the polarization of party and society which many predicted has not taken place. In *The New Class* I did not commit myself on this. *Both party and society are split from top to bottom by the same elements,* with cracks showing in the smallest corners. Freedom is also radiating from the Communist party—which, in truth, is not in fact Communist in the classic Leninist or Stalinist sense—radiating from its ranks of honest and thoughtful men.

This intellectual and social polarizing shows but one aspect of the desire of the Yugoslav peoples for greater administrative and economic autonomy. These aspirations are increasingly pronounced in all of the Yugoslav national communities, although among these the emphasis varies with the level of development and the past history and future prospects of each of them. In broad outline, the variations are: for the Slovenes, their ambitions lie mainly in the development of the economy; for the Croats, in state rights; for the Macedonians, in intellectual opportunities; for the Serbs, in two extremes—the preservation of the united country more or less as it is, and the desire for complete secession. It is not in keeping with the concept and scope of this book to

go in greater detail into the various individual aspirations of the Yugoslav peoples, or to examine closely
the nationalities question as a whole. Nevertheless,
certain singular features demand attention, both because of their novelty and because of their wider significance. The emancipation of the parties within each
republic, the separation of the administration of the republics from the federal administration, and the separation of the nationalities, each from each and each from
their center—here at the moment lies the most critical
aspect of disintegration within Yugoslavia. It should be
remembered that the Kingdom of Yugoslavia was
smashed in a few days of war in large part owing to the
dissensions among the nationalities. While the Communists got their new lease on life in uprisings against the
occupying forces—drawing on all Yugoslav peoples—yet
in their solution to the nationalities question they have
not, for all their fine words, gone very far beyond recognizing cultural and administrative autonomy. The old
Yugoslavia survived as a thoroughly Serbian centralist
monarchy, as a military-*cum*-police machine dominated
by the Serbs. And the new, Communist, Yugoslavia has,
in a different way, remained centralist through its single,
monolithic political party, which is also propped up by
an army and a secret police.

Although they are outside the historical category, the
national groups are, as said, variable in their aspirations
and potentialities, and their situations have changed
fundamentally. Yugoslavia was created by its peoples
and sustained in struggle against conquering empires—
first the Turkish and the Austrian, later the German and

the Italian. Now, except possibly the Soviet, there are no longer such empires to threaten it. Moreover, no one today disputes the right of even the most backward nation to protect its own statehood and national culture. With the weakening and destratification of the Communist party, not only are the forces that maintain Yugoslavia as a central state internally weakening, but also the very idea of Yugoslavism is being challenged, an idea carried by our forefathers through their long nationalist struggles and by my own generation, as revolutionaries, in the fight against the German and Italian occupiers.

But, though the idea of Yugoslavism is now evaporating before our eyes in spite of its having been the liveliest and most intense reality for many generations, it is no longer imperative for the life of Yugoslavia. As things are, the present Yugoslav regime is not, I am convinced, capable of surviving any major crisis, any more than the previous regime was. There is no equality among nationalities without human freedom, or without the genuine right of each national community to secession, the right to a self-contained economy and independent political organizations and its own armed forces. Only the vision of a new Yugoslavia within which national communities are associated by agreements as between sovereign states, and in which all citizens have political freedoms, offers any prospects for a more stable state community. The present regime has tried to stop, so far at least, any movement in that direction. It is possible that further ideological disintegration and an aggravation of social and nationality problems might well, in the event of a serious crisis, spur the ambitions of the military chiefs "to save the country," in spite of the fact that, because of the multinational character of the country, any military dictatorship is doomed to failure in Yugoslavia, as was King Alexander's in 1929.

In *The New Class* I put forward the thesis that a military dictatorship in a Communist country would represent an advance for the society. My presumption was that a military dictatorship would demolish the dogmatism and smash the monopoly of the party bureaucracy. But events in the Communist and the wider world have taken a direction that compels me to revise this view: the signs are that a military dictatorship, even in the Soviet Union, would curb democratic trends and aggravate the international situation. The example of Communism shows, to paraphrase Clemenceau, that the modern state and modern living conditions are too complex and too important to be left in the hands of generals.

Czechoslovakia is a drastic contemporary example of a simultaneous and interconnected eruption of the nationalities problem and the struggle for freedom. I believe that within the Soviet Union similar nationality grievances can erupt with democratic trends, the more so because the various national communities there have nothing approximating the rights enjoyed in Yugoslavia, for example. Yet this statement needs to be tempered with another: it would seem that trends toward freer social patterns and attitudes in the Soviet Union will not develop simultaneously with, or in the same way as, those in other East European countries. There are two reasons for this: democratic traditions in the Soviet

Union are weaker, and there is stagnation in its political bureaucracy and consequently in its world-power pretensions. Freedom in Eastern Europe depends a great deal upon trends within the Soviet Union, but freedom in the Soviet Union depends on trends in the whole world, not just in the Communist world.

Communism in Eastern Europe can no longer change conceptually. Nor can it, without great difficulty, rejuvenate any of the features of its administration, despite the fact that Communists spontaneously and consciously take refuge in deceiving themselves and others by proposing "far-reaching" measures "based on principle." Yugoslavia is the country where Communism has been most deeply affected by change, and indeed by disintegration; hence it is no accident that the most ingrained and entrenched beliefs in Yugoslavia should center on reorganization of the Communist League and on development of more rational methods of administration to deal with workers councils and the so-called "self-management" of enterprises. This last is supposed to provide the key to the door through which all troubles will vanish. It should be clear to any unclouded mind that no method of administration is in itself capable of exerting a major influence on social and property relationships unless it goes right to the heart of those relationships.

What did the reorganization of the Yugoslav Communist League and the development of "self-management" really mean? Each had its prehistory. In this thumbnail sketch of that history, the external factors I describe are inextricably mixed with my personal motives.

The fierceness of the struggle against Stalin and the monstrousness of his methods not only aroused distrust and disappointment among Yugoslav Communists—at least the most idealistic among them—but also spurred them on to strive for a society where such occurrences would be an impossibility. They sought a society that would have to be freer and more permissive toward critical opinions. Yet they remained dogmatists, and it was inevitable, in view of the forces that had produced them and the social realities in which they had fought, that any ideas and practical means which to their minds appeared different from Stalin's had *ipso facto* to become a more faithful interpretation and application of Marx's teaching. To reject Stalin, they had to reaffirm their Marxist faith. First of all, there was a return to Lenin, and, soon after that, to Marx. The most noticeable of "deviations" from Marx and Lenin was, naturally enough, the one that most deeply affected the Yugoslav Communists themselves. This "deviation" was the discrepancy between the Marxist-Leninist theory of the "withering away of the state" (after the seizure of power by the proletariat) and the real and continuing power of the Soviet state (which played an increasingly prominent role thirty years after the "proletariat" had seized power).

New attitudes had to be inculcated into the party, since it was the "fount and body of power" and more or less Stalinist—*i.e.,* founded on Stalin's "ideational unity" and on Lenin's "democratic centralism," which under Stalin had become another name for complete and nonquestioning obedience to the leadership, obedience, in effect, to one man. Efforts in Yugoslavia to achieve greater freedom inside the party and a different role for the party in society—with the emphasis to be on the effect of its ideas rather than on the effect of its giving orders—led the Communist party of Yugoslavia to change its name to the Yugoslav Communist League. This change of name was my idea. I had little trouble in persuading Kardelj as the Sixth Party Congress was approaching in the autumn of 1952. Together we telephoned Tito, who summoned us immediately. He, too, agreed immediately, and all the more readily when we reminded him that this was the name of Marx's first organization, for which he and Engels had written the *Communist Manifesto*. It is interesting to note that the party's new name came to me without my being conscious that Marx had used it for his organization and that I remembered this only later. This historical fact of course gave a tremendous boost to my confidence. Tito summoned Ranković, who disagreed with my proposal but, true to discipline, bowed to the opinion of the three of us. Then, as I remember, Tito eagerly snatched at an idea that Kardelj and I had spent hours thrashing out: we should have a multigroup, rather than a multiparty, system.

Nevertheless, as I pointed out earlier, democratization in the party, and consequently in the country, was curbed at the top. The tide of life, however, came to the party's rescue, because the party had been the initiator of that tide. Although they were thrust into the depths, "heretical," free opinions continued their creative activity and their struggles, individually and spontaneously;

and here the new name of the party, with other demo-cratic features and symbols born of the struggle against Stalinism, served as a rallying point and a *raison d'être*. It was as though the leaders were being reminded in a cautionary vision that they had once been revolution-aries, that they had once regarded themselves as demo-crats.

And now, fifteen years later, troubles are still afoot in the land. For the most part these are internal diffi-culties, which makes them crucial. The solutions that were before shunned and shut out are now foment-ing new forces more numerous and more self-reliant than before. The old party is now clinging to life in a welter of nostalgic memories and bureaucratic recrudes-cences. The leadership remains more or less the same, and to this day is intransigent in its insistence on trying to resolve matters of life and death for the public and the country by means of a "new" reorganization of the Yugoslav Communist League, this time with a more vigo-rous shake-up of the perplexed and discouraged rank and file over such matters as counterfeit ideas and fossil-ized formulas. In effect, the issue is the leadership's own power.

Just what is Yugoslavia's program of "self-manage-ment"? What are the prospects of its finding a solution to the social and nationality troubles now besetting Yugoslavia?

The idea of self-management was conceived by Kardelj and me, with some help from our comrade Kidrič. Soon after the outbreak of the quarrel with Stalin, in 1949, as far as I remember, I began to reread Marx's *Capital,* this time with much greater care, to see if I could find the answer to the riddle of why, to put it in simplistic terms, Stalinism was bad and Yugoslavia was good. I discovered many new ideas and, most interesting of all, ideas about a future society in which the immediate producers, through free association, would themselves make the decisions regarding production and distribution—would, in effect, run their own lives and their own future.

The country was in the stranglehold of the bureaucracy, and the party leaders were in the grip of rage and horror over the incorrigibly arbitrary nature of the party machine they had set up and that kept them in power. One day—it must have been in the spring of 1950—it occurred to me that we Yugoslav Communists were now in a position to start creating Marx's free association of producers. The factories would be left in their hands, with the sole proviso that they should pay a tax for military and other state needs "still remaining essential." With all this, I felt a twinge of reservation: is not this a way for us Communists, I asked myself, to shift the responsibility for failures and difficulties in the economy onto the shoulders of the working class, or to compel the working class to take a share of such responsibilities from us? I soon explained my idea to Kardelj and Kidrič while we sat in a car parked in front of the villa where I lived. They felt no such reservation, and I was able all too easily to convince them of the indisputable harmony between my ideas and Marx's teaching. Without leaving the car, we thrashed it out for little more than half an hour. Kardelj thought it was a good idea, but one that should not be put into effect for another five or six years, and Kidrič agreed with him. A couple of days later, however, Kidrič telephoned me to say that we were ready to go ahead at once with the first steps. In his impulsive way he began to elaborate and expound on the whole conception. A little later, a meeting was held in Kardelj's cabinet office with the trade-union leaders, and they proposed the abolition of the workers councils, which up to that time had functioned only as consultative bodies for the management. Kardelj suggested that my proposals for management should be associated with the workers councils, first of all in a way that would give them more rights and greater responsibilities. Shortly there began the debates on the issues of principle and on the statutory aspects, preparations that went on for some four or five months. Tito, busy with other duties and absent from Belgrade, took no part in this and knew nothing of the proposal soon to introduce a workers council bill in the parliament until he was informed by Kardelj and me in the government lobby room during a session of the National Assembly. His first reaction was: our workers are not ready for that yet! But Kardelj and I, convinced that this was an important step, pressed him hard, and he began to unbend as he paid more attention to our explanations. The most important part of our case was that this would be the beginning of democracy, something that socialism had not yet achieved; further, it could be plainly seen by the world and the international workers' movement as a radical departure from Stalinism. Tito paced up and down, as though completely wrapped in his own thoughts. Suddenly he stopped and exclaimed: "Factories belonging to the workers—something that has never yet been achieved!" With these words, the theories worked out by Kardelj and myself seemed to shed their complications, and seemed, too, to find better prospects of being workable. A few months later, Tito explained the Workers' Self-Management Bill to the National Assembly.

These reminiscences are beginning to make me feel like one of those old-fashioned politicians who has "heard it all said ages ago," who "said exactly the same thing" on such and such an occasion. But I take comfort that my reminiscences are not really as bad as that from what I now know. Even if the course of action to which I committed myself had been applied consistently in the party and in the management of the economy—that is, to society as a whole—it would at the best have led only to a confrontation with the basic problems a little more rapidly and perhaps in an aggravated form. It would not have solved the basic problems, for it would not have been able to extricate the system itself from utopian practices and practical coercion. What in fact happened was the start of new dogma formulation and myth making, as if the survival of the human race, or at least of the Communists, depended on this. Here, whatever other merits I may claim, I cannot escape my share of the blame in creating this new dogma and myth.

More important is the fact that the whole of the subsequent course of events in Yugoslavia shows that the precise role of the party, or form of the administration, though these have to be determined, is less important than freedom for trends and currents of ideas in the party and freedoms for society itself. For fifteen years there hovered over the workers councils the continuing presence of the all-powerful secret police, and this went on until the Central Committee plenary session on Brioni in the summer of 1966, when the secret-police chiefs were dismissed. In spite of the persistent assurances that the role of the party is predominantly ideological, its undemocratic structure and its privileged position over society still remain. Furthermore, fear of the secret police has not disappeared, although its methods are milder and its powers considerably reduced; and during 1968 party leaders were asked to "revolutionize" and strengthen the Communist League on the basis of a "unanimous platform"—in other words, secret control over the public is still not forbidden and punishable, nor are minority rights defined and guaranteed within the party.

The workers councils and other self-management bodies have been unable, by virtue of either their mandate or their actual position in society, to solve the problems of a free and harmonious development for the economy, or even the problem of equitable distribution (the so-called distribution according to work performed). This is not possible without statutory guarantees for free and active participation by ordinary people, first and foremost those at work, and also freedom for independent trade unions and other organizations, the right to strike and to demonstrate, and so on. The economy may be regarded as man's war against nature, and as such it demands greater discipline the more complicated the working conditions and the more sophisticated the equipment that has to be handled. In spite of their good intentions, the workers councils, with their primitiveness and their patriarchal leadership, and their merely ostensible democracy, are often a cause of disorder, inefficiency, and illusionism. The consequences for the economy are all the more severe because the role played by the federal government and the governments of the republics in planning and development is less prominent today, and much more inefficient, than in any Western country. Even if the workers councils were not led and controlled by party members, even if they were free from the pressures of bureaucrats within industry and in the local authorities, the very fact that their activity does not step beyond the framework of a single firm, and that firm's production and distribution, means that they are not solving, and cannot solve, a single one of the key questions of society and of the nation. Politics are an argument about life's itinerary and about life itself, about the destiny of a nation; and they involve the banding together of people; hence it follows that an unfree people can have no scope in the cells of the economic organism. If the revolutionary and democratic Communists have been looking to the workers councils and to self-management for an escape from the bugbears of Stalinism, they ignore the reality that the party bureaucrats and oligarchs, too, have their vested interests in these organizations.

Here is a description of this other side of self-management:

"It is proclaimed that the severe limitations placed on the power of the bureaucracy have led to an 'enlargement of the material base of self-management' that came into being as a result of the redistribution of the national income. It has been said that the 'work organization' now has its 'hands freed' so that it can manage itself. Apart from this, there is no major change in social relationships; and there is a perfectly logical reason for this. The bureaucracy has benevolently 'dropped the income into the work organization's lap'; but such 'benevolence' could be seen in a different light. Let us suppose the Lord of the Manor has distributed part of his lands among numerous landless laborers on condition that they pay him an annual tithe. He accompanies his gesture with philanthropic clichés about voluntarily impoverishing himself. The serfs, each on his own plot of land, which is fertile or barren according to his luck, transform themselves into free-working men capable of managing their own lives. They have now been brought into a situation where they no longer have anyone or anything to complain about: now they themselves are responsible for their poverty; and out of their meager income they themselves have to buy their implements and seed, and, of course, to pay the philanthropic landlord his tithe. And he, for his part, with his lands diminished, has been reduced to nothing less than ownership of a wealthy estate. His power over the land that has been divided up and parceled out is no less than it was before. He takes his share of the produce from this land and uses it for upkeep and development of the estate that still remains in his own hands. In this situation the 'more radical' of the smallholders see the solution to their problems in a reduction of their payments to the landlord, while the completely 'revolutionary' ones consider that the entire estate should be broken up and parceled out. They see in this a guarantee of equitable relationships, freedom for the individual, and even successful husbandry. The point here is not that the serfs by becoming 'free' smallholders achieve no real change in their social situation, but that proprietorship has gone, leaving the landless laborer to manage things as a whole, working himself within that whole." [1]

The bitter ring of truth from these lines is not diminished by the old-fashioned solutions that are hinted at and that the writer recommends in an oblique way; these are founded on a myth that has proved abortive in some areas and has been exploded in others—the mythical belief in the revolutionary ethos of the working class as such, and in the abolition of ownership as a panacea. But this by no means suggests that the scarcely more than incipient and tentative forms of so-called workers' management have not been, or cannot be, a useful device for siphoning off dogmatism and keeping bureaucratic arbitrariness under control. Even if they are in some respects an effective and always a convenient shelter for party bureaucrats and demagogues, they are also a refuge for democratic-minded individuals and for groups setting trends in the war against arbitrariness and injustice in enterprises, for those who defend democratic outlooks and expectations. The forms of so-called workers' management *can* be used as a handhold by those who identify socialism with social justice and human freedom.

1. Milan Mirić, "Reservations for Word and Action," *Razlog,* Zagreb, 1967, Vol. VII, No. 2–3.

The same possibility holds true for other features of Communism in East European countries today, provided that new people come along with new ideas and new ways and means.

PART THREE

MEANS AS ENDS

I

Emphatic in my mind, as I recount my reflections on the nature and course of Communism during a period of more than fifteen years, is this fact: what interests me is not so much the triumph of my own ideas, but the actual course of the struggle. Because triumph, as I remember and as I know, is coercive and intoxicating, and consequently self-seeking and unbridled. But my own experience tells me that my lack of enthusiasm for victory is simple neither in concept nor in motivation; for me, victory is only a continuation of the struggle, only a discovery of the possibilities for further struggle. Ideas that do not take root, that are not the heart and soul of human existence are not genuine ideas. Since man finds no peace in the cessation of ordeal, there can never be enough of struggle, victory, and power.

That is why I cannot and will not, though I have now reached a stage where I could, spend my remaining days in the comfortable glow of being regarded as a rebel who endured, even as a morally triumphant one. It is not quite clear to me which of the two phrases prevails—"I cannot" or "I will not." Is it that I cannot because my conscience warns that a retreat into an ideological or other intellectual wilderness would be treachery to myself and to all who are sympathetic to my ideas or who have helped me in my resistance? Or is it that I will not because of sheer defiance and because of an irremediable craving for power or glory—for the prolongation of my ordeal, for my "place in history"? Or can it be, perhaps, that this relentless, intractable craving to go on, to go further, is the result of certain kinds of conscience? For if I have long known that the fight for ideas of any kind is at the same time a fight for some definite form of power and domination over others, it must be also clear to me that the idea, the idea as idea, the idea in embryo, is at the same time the embryo of the struggle for power, the embryo of power itself.

The ideas I mean are, of course, political and social ideas. But the same thing is true for any idea if it is seen through a broad spectrum and without sophistry. The idea and the deed are indivisible, because an idea is always an idea of a deed, an idea of creation; and every new deed, every act of creation, leaves about it a desert and exerts its power and domination over disordered and unfledged forces and relationships.

Franz Kafka thought the human race was condemned before committing an offense; people were condemned for just being people. It is no accident that at a time when liberals and empiricists considered socialism to be a harebrained adventure and a childish utopia, and when at the same time the socialists themselves considered it the "finally discovered," "scientifically proved" system of brotherhood, of equality, "tried out in practice," Kafka described to his friend Max Brod, if I am not mistaken, how, during the processions of a workers' demonstration, he could just make out at the rear of the march the leaders, of both sexes, the secretaries and the committee members—all of them future masters of the society of the enraptured and courageous crowds. The story of power is told and retold. The misfortunes of a dismembered Renaissance Italy, with the starkness of the struggle for power among its princes, provided source material for the sensitive and profound thinker Niccolò Machiavelli, in particular for his *Discorsi*, a tragic view of man's fate in society as it then was.

Society, simply because it is a community of different strata and forces, with different aspirations and views, is not viable without an authority, and the authority cannot come into existence and maintain itself without struggle—a struggle employing ideas among suitable means. All other tales are inane, all other solaces futile. Those who preach politics and project a society without authority live, at best, a life of illusions; and those who maintain that they can live without a political attitude have either submitted to one or acquiesce in one. For Aristotle, a man outside the polis (city-state, society) could be imagined only as a god or a beast; but today, although we have not progressed much farther in our knowledge of the gods than did the men of his age, we do know that there is no extrasocial animal. Contemporary man's lack of interest in politics, or, more accurately, his refusal to become interested in them, is inscribed with the mark of society and the fateful division of the world. On the one hand, in multiparty systems some people maintain that the machinery of society can go on running somehow without them, and others say that their own activity makes not the slightest difference to the part played by whatever party, whether incoming or outgoing, they happen to support. On the other hand, in one-party systems people are politically passive simply because politics do not exist for them once the top party leaders have taken over the monopoly of political life. Politics constitute man's existence in his own social and national community, and the community's existence inside other communities, and it is no more possible to escape from the community than it is from life or death. Passiveness in politics is a surrender to the dictates and mercies of "higher powers." The choice between one policy and another is, finally, an option for means; and means are the only reliable yardstick by which to measure the values of the ideas under whose name the means are employed and of the leaders who employ them.

As I write these lines, the streets of Paris and West Berlin, and many university towns in the United States, are alive with the furor of angry young intellectuals protesting against many modern establishments, among them the "welfare state," with its scarcely distinguishable political parties, with its standardized production and its overprudent freedoms. Similar occurrences took place recently in the streets of Warsaw and Prague against the unprogressive dogmas of national leaders and the subordination of national interests to the Soviet "elder brother." Although the immediate causes and objectives of these movements are different, they have a great deal in common. Both reveal that the compelling necessity, complexity, and massiveness of modern technology is augmenting the ranks of the intellectual class, making it more independent and important in society than ever before. Young people are being gripped by visions of a world that embodies their own conception and is more humane—a world that has not been emasculated and lacerated by ideologies or disenfranchised by poverty and despotism or dishonored by racial and ideological discrimination, a world that is spared strategic wars like that in Vietnam and allied aggression against peaceful sovereign states like Czechoslovakia.

These newly kindled fires of youth have aroused and in turn are being fanned by other ideological and political forces. These forces are more marked and cohesive in the West, where they have acquired or adopted a name, the "New Left," which has at the same time aroused suspicions and revealed truths that cannot be easily dismissed.

With the revival of liberalism, the black flag of Bakunin's and Blanqui's anarchism, after a whole century of oblivion, has been raised from the dusts of history to overshadow the red flag, which, in its turn, has become part of the decoration of juridical, parliamentary, even ecclesiastical insignia. The spirit of revolution, of unrest

and discontent, has been aroused, as has happened before, at a time when the general situation seemed quiet
and calm, with the standard of living rising and the rule
of law growing stronger. But the soullessness of profit-
making industry and the grayness of welfare as a single
ultimate ideal—especially when regarded with the accommodations that the Communists in the West are
making with parliamentary life and the transformation
of Communists into a new class in the East—have
aroused this discontent and conscious resentment among
so-called radical groups. Various trends have joined and
merged in the course of an onslaught on contemporary
society. Naïve groups of existentialists, beatniks, and
hippies have maintained only a nonconformist exterior,
while the Communist and anarchist factions have tried
to convert student discontent with old-fashioned educational methods and the lack of recognition for intellectual attainments into an onslaught on the regime itself.

A radical opposition inside and outside government is
a vital necessity for every society, even if it does no
more than provide an impetus to move against stagnation, a corrective to errors, and a warning to slumbering
consciences. The present-day radicalism of youth varies
from country to country, but one can, I think, speak of
an "extranational" New Left. No sensible person will
deny that the New Left has set its seal on this historical
moment by jerking the established powers out of the
mire, by shaking belief in the electronic paradise of technology—and, less obviously in the East, by unmasking
the privilege-seeking nature of official Communism.

(I had just put these observations down on paper

when, on June 2, 1968, the student demonstrations erupted in Belgrade. This gave me a deeper and sharper insight into the New Left. Although the demonstrations broke out more or less spontaneously, as a revolt against police actions, there had been noted earlier a certain discontent among students and nonconformist academics. Oppositionist trends had appeared in theoretical periodicals. The movement spread to other universities, embracing a completely representative cross section of the student body, including a considerable proportion of Communists. The mood and outlook of the student body and many of the staff have been indisputably democratic socialist. Egalitarian and puritanical slogans and the display of pictures of Che Guevara were an expression of the desire to keep the movement somehow within the bounds of legality. This being so, the student leaders only caused confusion and isolated the movement, particularly since the regime soon adopted these same slogans and promised to meet the students' demands. Being without firm leadership, and being isolated from the workers, who were more concerned with their own hardships owing to their low wages than with any "role" ordained for them by "history," the movement fizzled out. Yet neither students nor dissident members of the teaching staff displayed any severe signs of demoralization. Their first conscious and planned mass political outburst has strengthened confidence in the opportunities for fighters for freedom of thought and for a freer, more equitable society.)

These, then, appear to be the frontiers of the New Left. Even its name reveals that its origins lie more in its loyalty to the revolution that was betrayed by the "classic" Communist leftists than in any new appraisal of political ideals or in the discovery of practicable ways of achieving them. This is understandable. The New Left is, in fact, composed of numerous factions that have sprung from the ruins of the world creed of Communism, or, more accurately, from the disappointment with Communism as a stabilized class society and the resentment against the accommodations made by Western Communist parties in their attitudes to national particularities and to the environment of a modern industrial state. Merely by remaining intransigent in their rejection of existing relationships and institutions, the New Left was able at one time to carry through demonstrations without any clear program, and even without some sort of stable organization and self-conscious leadership. But in committing itself to the Communist and anarchist intellectual heritage, it could not do for long without an ideology. So there are obvious reasons why some of its adherents should have discovered and accepted, at least for the time being, Herbert Marcuse's findings on the conditions of the working class in relation to modern industrial society and his belief in a society that would give man freedom and felicity by removing the barriers to his libido.

It is the old, old story with a different twist.

The New Left shows its latent ambitions by indifference, even impatience, with respect to "revisionist," *i.e.,* democratic-socialist, ideas and trends in Communist systems and even to "unpolitical" students who are naïve enough to identify themselves with the New Left movement. The ordeals of independent-minded people and the repression of youth in the East lie upon the consciousness of the New Left in the West. So, a warranted show of gratitude to the New Leftists does not require anyone to be so enraptured as to fail to notice certain of its tendencies. One notes their fanatical militancy, their tendency to engage in relentless factional infighting in struggles for principle. One can discern in these the embryos of ideological parties. Nor can one ignore, in the preaching of a Rudolf Dutschke, or in the ingenuity of a Fritz Teufel, or in the bravado of a Daniel Cohn-Bendit, the masks of a domination over society that may be yet to come. This observation is not a belittlement of the intellectual revolutionaries, or of the human qualities of these current movements. It is merely a pointer to their other side, an incontrovertible one—their authoritarianism, the violent methods employed to make a reality of their ideologies, and their attempts to devise ideologies that are all things to all men.

It is extremely important that every man of ideas, every fighter, democrat and humanist, whether in the West or in the East, should realize that this is true, because it is a warning about the dark and mundane side of "consummate" ideas and "ultimate deeds," and reveals their practical and practicable side. Furthermore, each idea comes to reality in the muddy torrent of life; it does so with a crudity that seems to increase in inverse proportion to its efforts to remain pure, and it seems to become more tarnished as the leaders more completely identify their own destiny with it, their own lusts, ambitions, way of life, and their so-called responsibility to history. By being banished from ideas man does not cease to be the slave of his own attributes. In history, many are the revolutionaries, and indeed other politicians, who have lost their sense of proportion because of their personal ambitions. Those men who are in tune with the definition and limits of the idea itself have been very rare. Knowing this will not automatically rescue anything or teach anyone a lesson, because what is incapable of surviving will not survive, and none is so ignorant as he who will not learn. Yet to know this can help fighters and men of ideas to remain awake to their own qualities, to be on the alert against the corruptions inherent in power; to respect the law rather than take it into their own hands, to have greater respect for human beings than for abstractions, to be more concerned with common human needs than with their own historical record. Fighters who fail to become aware of this easily fall prey to their own ideals and the manipulations of their superiors. And the statesmen who fail to understand that their power represents, in some measure at least, a betrayal of their ideas, since these ideas can only have come to fruition in a practicable, which is to say nonideal, way, easily sink into the exercise of authoritarianism.

As for myself, however much I may secretly crave power, I hope with all my heart that this cup will pass from me and that I shall remain safely ensconced in the original, toil-worn innocence of my ideas. This, then, is the dilemma in which I live and meditate and fight. Reverses, strangely enough, do not aggravate my dilemma; rather, they diminish it. Under adversity, I am more and more under the urging to resolve my dilemma by materializing my ideas, by relating idea and deed. Further-more, although I feel confident that there would be im-measurably more human freedom in the system for which I am fighting than there is at present, I am aware that in the very nature of things falsehoods, corruption, and self-seeking would be bound to flourish at the inception of such a system. No one can doubt that Tito's successor will take over direction of a state that is disunited and neglected, and that may be abandoned to the cupidity of Soviet pan-Russian imperialism. Yet these unidealist challenges and difficulties spur and guide my energies toward power—toward the materialization of ideas, to-ward duty, toward glory. Thus a man achieves freedom in his ideas—in his deeds—but he is thereby committed to being their slave.

To forestall any misunderstanding that this exposi-tion is somehow a cunningly camouflaged way of con-cealing my own unidealistic motives, I will divulge that not even the materialization of my ideas, although this has been limited to public declaration, has come about in an unadulterated ideal way. I maintain that this con-fession has value if for no other reason than as a docu-ment about people and the times—about the painful and tragic separation of a Communist from dogma and power. I am, after all, obligated to make it, since many people remember, though probably no one fully under-stands, my former "recantation" and "inconsistencies."

As I have already explained, at the end of 1953 I fore-saw my fall from power and the way of sorrows ahead. Moreover, I foresaw the actual shape that the feud and campaigns against me would assume. I was not unaware of the fates of many party members who had fallen by the wayside, and, indeed, I had played a part in deciding the fate of such people. My picture of what was to come, my personal knowledge, and my determination were certainly a help to me in undergoing the days of reckoning which began in January 1954 with the convocation of the Third Plenum of the Yugoslav Communist League, which had my "revisionism" as its agenda. The actual ordeal was to be much more frightening and painful than anything I had sensed or could foresee. This plenary session was different from my other trials. All the later court sessions in which I was the defendant were mockeries of justice, though not, of course, as terrifying as those staged by Stalin, first in the U.S.S.R. and later elsewhere in Eastern Europe, in order to rid himself of awkward opponents and crush even the slightest suspicion of opposition. Yet my trials served a similar purpose: they were calculated to remove an incorrigible "daydreamer" and to intimidate people in high places, who were already frightened. As a matter of fact, on a point of law, which was written into the statutes and was binding on the party, my plenum trial was illegal, both as regards the procedure by which Tito and his colleagues manufactured a "majority" and a "united front" in the Central Committee, and in respect of the act that was being investigated.

At this session it was revisionism that was on trial and being "judged," a revisionism whose origins in Yugoslavia were twofold: first, opposition to the identification of Communist parties—in this case the Yugoslav Communist League—with the Leninism of the Communist party of the Soviet Union, an identification that produced and nurtured its own particular brand of pro-Soviet "fifth column"; and second, opposition to Stalinist "ideational party unity," since that was actually the ideational form of personal and oligarchical authority in the party and state, and the umbrella under which it sheltered. From the ideational framework of Tito's resistance to Stalin, Yugoslav revisionism started to reject his "monolithic party unity" as well, as being a variant of ideological, Marxist-Leninist monopoly in the party and state. That is why this plenum was (and is) considered both outside and inside Yugoslavia as a stoppage, even as a step back, in the democratization of the party, and consequently of the country. In my memory and in my being it has remained to this day a most shameless show of force and an insufferable infamy.

That is the true nature of that plenum; and that is how I felt while it was in session, indeed how I have felt ever since it was convened.

I have never at any time been, or wished to be, in collusion with anyone; nor had I then acted against either the party or the government. And least of all had I caused any offense to my comrades, except that I had been so bold as to put forward, or, rather, I had been unable to help expressing, my own reflections on a certain society and my own proposals for improving matters. Moreover, the party and government were my party and my government, too, and Tito was a person whom I respected and a leader whom I recognized, in spite of an arbitrariness that I never found comfortable and despite the differences in our views, which were always apparent. However, the witch hunt against me got under way and the leaden slabs of a boycott were boxed around me before the formal verdict of the plenum had been delivered.

But in spite of my perspicacity and my anticipation of what was going to happen to me, I did make a partial recantation at the end of the plenary session. I could not escape paying my debt to the dogma to which I was committed and to the movement that had a claim on me, because my activities until then, my whole way of life, were registered in its records.

Why did this happen, and how did it happen?

Between the institution of proceedings against me in the party secretariat, which led to the convocation of the Central Committee Plenum, and the beginning of the session, on January 15, 1954, there was an interval of fifteen days, and during this period I did not get more than an hour's sleep a night. I was exhausted and drained dry, but still in command of my faculties. People looked at me aghast, as though I had just come down from the gallows—such horrified expressions I was to encounter for years afterward. My first good night's sleep came at the end of the first day of the session, on the eve of my "recantation"; and I can only conclude that this act was forced upon me in my sleep, unless falling asleep was itself the result of a subconscious decision to do it.

At a meeting I had a couple of days before the session with the top party leaders (Tito, Kardelj, and Ranković), Tito indirectly suggested that I should take party unity into consideration. During the actual session Kardelj informed me that Tito's view was that now my case had to be settled, but that in five or six months' time a more lenient attitude toward me would be taken. But I do not believe that either of these incidents could possibly have affected my conduct to any crucial extent.

There was no one beside me except my wife, Štefanija-Štefica. She tried to convince me I was wrong when I told her I would have to make a sacrifice of my views to some extent, and though she was sufficiently firm, she was too tender and considerate to succeed in dissuading me. During all this time I was not only lonely, but also abandoned, rejected, and despised. All the Central Committee members who until then had let me know they were with me now turned away from me with loathing and contempt, and those who had given me encouragement made bitter denunciations of me, one after the other, at the plenary session. The only exceptions, the only people to give me any support at the session, were Mitra Mitrović, my first wife, and Vladimir Dedijer, each in a different way and for different reasons. Though I had made no arrangement with Mitra, I had complete faith in her. Later, under pressures of various sorts, she became disillusioned with politics and devoted herself to educational and literary activities. Dedijer spent quite a lot of time with me in this period; but, caught in my web of suspicion, I did not trust him—I thought he had been sent to spy on me. At the plenum he was firmer than I was, but soon after he began to keep his distance, for reasons that even today are not completely clear to me, though it was evident from the beginning that he was going his own way, a way that has led him, finally, to a position where he can work as a historian more or less free from interference.

I felt no physical fear, but I was anxious about the fate of people inclined to my way of thinking who were disturbed by the sentence passed on me. I had heard that the secret police had already begun to draw up lists of "Djilasites," and I could not banish from my mind the memory of what had happened to the earlier opposition, the Stalinist opposition. They had been thrown into concentration camps and subjected to brutal treatment and monstrous intellectual and moral pressures. I knew from the reactions to my published articles that there were many people all over the country who were on my side, but they were unorganized and unprepared, so that I had alone to bear the responsibilities. This was a serious cause for concern and a heavy burden on my conscience, and it forced me to make a withdrawal which, in the particular conditions and circumstances, could only appear as a renunciation, at least a partial one, of declared ideas. From this it can be seen that my act of "recantation" contained elements of politically motivated tactics, even stratagems.

But even this was not decisive. The fateful crux of the matter lay in my emotional attitude. I continued to feel that I was a Communist, albeit hesitant about certain dogmas, that I was bound body and soul to the Communist party. Like the heretics of days gone by, like the sundry oppositionists in the Stalin trials, I proved my loyalty to the ideology and to the party by recantation.

My feelings as I was making my formal "recantation" were a mixture of disappointment and disgust with myself and with the "star-chamber" tribunal, and with the ideology and with the fact that it had ever been created. But there was also a certain diabolical delight in this self-humiliation, particularly because it was an illustration and an endorsement of the mutilation of a human being on the wheel of ideology, and, even more, because the victim was until recently a comrade and a colleague of the prosecutors. The scene was rather like that at one of Stalin's purge trials, toned down by circumstances rather than by the good intentions of the judges. It lacked only the penitent, and I relished the thought that I could fit the bill with my "recantation," especially because the stage managers were obviously much concerned that they should not be considered Stalinists. Nevertheless, I did not burn all my flimsy and unfinished bridges. I did not renounce my philosophical views; nor did I admit that there was anything discreditable in my motives.

I realized all the time that I was losing a historic battle —that I was no match for my greatest moment, perhaps my only historic moment. But I also knew that I had not submitted, and that I would gather all my strength in the new, changed circumstances. I sensed, I was even certain, that people with ideas similar to mine would interpret my "recantation," at worst, as a bad tactical move and *not* as a renunciation of my ideas. That was the true position: neither then nor later did I meet anyone prepared to believe that I had really recanted, even though my "recantation" benefited adversaries—who used it to combat my influence—no less than vacillating supporters, who found in it an excuse for breaking away and going over to the other side. At the end of the session, Tito went to the lengths of making this pointed remark: "We shall see how far Djilas has sincerely repented." This I regard as the acme of callousness and duplicity, but it was, at the same time, a source of fresh resistance and resentment within me.

The penalty meted out to me was worse than the humiliation and resentment I felt. The commission that had been set up to recommend the penalty and show due process for it was not a random combination. It was headed by Vladimir Bakarić, presumably because his opinions were close to mine. By undertaking a responsibility imposed upon him, he, like many others, discredited his own ideas. On behalf of the commission, he recommended, with the agreement of Tito and the other leaders, a penalty imposed on me of severe reprimand, with final warning. But some of the other members of the party tribunal, from rage or rancor were seized by the passionate desire to have me expelled from the party. Tito intervened. I ought not to be expelled, he presumably argued, because the Western press might interpret this as a Stalinist method of dispensing justice. So I was to remain in the party under the most shameful conditions, in sackcloth and ashes, partly to protect the regime's reputation at a time of its need for economic aid from the West.

These events were ordeals, but they were a lesson, too. Intellectual and moral viability was only possible in isolation from a real-life situation such as this, from a party and an ideology like these. Those who remained, who kept their place, doomed themselves to decay, to the all-too-frequent renunciations of their opinions and personality, to continual compromise, to sycophancy. Delimitation of the situation, coming to terms with it, with party and ideology, with my own past and my own self—these to me were the condition and aspect of forthcoming wise and creative endeavors.

No one from the top party hierarchy sought any contact with me (nor have they from that day to this), although the suggestion was made known to me that I might take some steps to re-establish relations to some degree. I opted for solitude, for the depths of forgetfulness—but also for a withdrawal of my "recantation." Two months later I submitted my resignation from the party. This was my first public gesture, the first deliberate sign of my refusal to compromise. From that time forth I lived, for months, even years, obsessed with my plenum "recantation" and under the fear that pressures were to be used to make me renounce my writings and my ideas. During my first imprisonment (1956–1961) I even lived in fear that drugs might be used to destroy my will and make me repent. I felt the need constantly to seek approval, to prove myself to myself and to others— in suffering. It was not until my second imprisonment (1962–1966) that I mastered these fears and weaknesses. My jailers were also aware of this, and, when at the end of 1966 they no longer found it worthwhile keeping me in prison, they released me unconditionally. I had no foreknowledge that such a move was afoot.

Hence there seems little point in mentioning "my" submission of the request "on the basis" of which I was released conditionally in 1961. This is what happened at that time. The prison administration had been making direct and indirect attempts to secure my submissiveness and a change of heart. When I threatened to break off any further attempts at discussion, they sent to me Slobodan Penezić, a Central Committee member and a high official in the secret police, who gave me a ready-prepared request to sign. There was one sentence in the request that could have been interpreted as recognition by me that my assertions had been falsified by the facts of real life. Nevertheless, I signed the document. I realized that the state leaders needed it for future blackmail, and this later proved to be the case, but my literary and other plans made it essential for me to get out of prison. I did not find that what I had done lay heavily upon me; in myself I remained unflinching, although tortured by doubts and fears that my action would be misunderstood.

After my rearrest, on April 7, 1962, for another five years of imprisonment, all this became part of the past, though it remained indelible and intransient.

There is, finally, another, still more unsavory, side to the story of my ideas and their expression in the real world. Forced into a situation where I had to keep silent, where I had to submit to being "killed by silence," as one of the party leaders put it after they had started to settle their score with me, I was compelled to approach the Western press and Western publishers because no one else was prepared to publish my statements and books. In doing this I knew that I was exposing myself to the risk of being called a "servile pawn," a "mercenary," a "Bevanite," or even a "C.I.A. appendage," by the Yugoslav regime. Similar and even worse labels had been smeared on me as early as the time of the plenum trial, before I had begun to think about what I was going to do with myself and before I had contemplated writing the books that were published years later. I also knew that my statements and my writings, once published, would be exploited by people and forces whose motives were different from, even opposed to, mine.

I was unable to create for myself the river in which I had to swim; I had to swim or remain on a riverbank that was not mine. I swam off, without recoiling from the slanders and smears, for I felt there were no grounds for them, either in my inner self or in my intentions.

Today such a step seems straightforward and easy to me. But at that time it was not, when the Cold War was raging, when in Yugoslavia the Communist League was still engrossed with the internal "purge" and with dangers from abroad, and when public opinion was confined and subdued. Support from intellectuals and the man in the street, although I was aware of its existence, was indeterminate, sporadic, and incohesive. I was on my own. That was how it had to be. I had then, I have now, no complaints, no regrets, because I was forging my own destiny by myself. I saw no other way but this way through the wilderness, through the mire and undergrowth. The thought behind everything that I wrote at that time, everything that I had felt the need to demonstrate, with all my heart, in my own life, can be reduced to this: people, my country's sons, should not be humiliated and persecuted because of ideas, for expressing their thoughts. I am not persuaded that this can be achieved among human beings soon, if ever. But the struggle for it is worthwhile; it is inevitable—in the same way that evil may seem ineradicable but can be rooted out.

And who knows, if there were no evil inside us, whether we should be the beings that we are. Should we then be able, should we then know how, to drive the creative, the godlike, powers within ourselves?

II

I may readily overtax the reader with laments because of the suffering and distress that my mind had to overcome before it was emancipated from a doctrinaire violation of its being and from dreams of an ideal society. But my book is committed—and I hope my readers are as well—to this account to the last sentence because the ways and means by which I made my breakthrough are in many respects characteristic of the opinions and destiny of creative thinkers living in Communist systems. As such they are, I believe, significant and instructive for the moral and emotional content, quite untainted by political motives.

Thus, all my doubts, speculations, and vexations are dwarfed by vacillation over the choice of ways and means for the struggle inside Communism.

My reverses were the harder to bear because I had emerged in my mature years from a war-torn and insurrection-riven country, while from my early youth I had been familiar with the ways of revolution and violence. In addition, I spent some considerable time in power, something to which most people, perhaps, are not frantically attracted, but which, once it has been savored, poisons everyone with its lotuslike sweetness, divine or diabolic, or, most probably, a little of both.

True, the secret police from the beginning of my open conflict with the party leadership in January 1954, if not before that, began an unremitting espionage against me. My apartment was wire-tapped. I was openly followed wherever I went, and pressures were put on anyone who approached me, even in the street. I was completely isolated, and my opportunities for any sort of activity were destroyed, even had I had a clearer, more definite idea of what could be done. I grasped at my only remaining resource, which was to work out my ideas and to write my autobiography, and this imposed itself as the most important thing that could be done. I went on with this in prison, together with my main form of self-expression, which I was more readily allowed to engage in—writing short stories and novels.

But neither inside nor outside prison was I able to rid myself of my ponderings on the most suitable, the most practicable forms and methods of struggle against the party oligarchy's despotism and monopoly. According to whether I was feeling bitter or elated, two extremes forced themselves upon me—rebellion and a *coup d'état,* or legal opposition in the press and in the party. For the most part, these were momentary thoughts; for my desire and my realization of the need for a gradual reformist change of Communism, at least in my own country, became increasingly firmly lodged in my mind. Meanwhile, my former comrades made it impossible for me to engage in any public activities. They expunged my name from the roll of the past. They tried to wreck my family. They used the smear that for thirty pieces of silver I had sold state secrets to foreign powers. They threw me in jail for two periods totaling nine years—the first term to satisfy their own ideological reasons, and the second term to avoid giving offense to the Soviet government, to prove they showed no leniency toward my "anti-Soviet outbursts." But my resentment and animosity, however much they may have boiled up in my moments of humiliation and bitterness, never succeeded for long in clouding my mind, or in changing the conviction that had been forming inside me from the beginning—that democracy was the way out of Communism's vicious circle. Nor did I deviate from the path that I had discovered at the beginning, that of changing Communism by nonviolent means. I did not yield to any vindictive passion to pay anyone back in the same coin, because from my mother's lap it had been inculcated into me that those who humiliate and torture others are in fact demonstrating their own worthless and twisted natures. In essence my dispute with the party arose from my realization that ideas by themselves do not make men either sublime or worthless, but that it is the means they employ that make them one or the other.

That is how I proved to myself, and inside myself, my own constancy—something my adversaries, bogged down in routine and up to their ears in the ecstasies of power, have never been able to understand, let alone to emulate. My past has not been all taken up with revolution and violence; idealism and humanity are part of it, too. Moreover, in the same way that I had joined the revolutionary movement and resorted to violent methods in the belief that they were indispensable in this wicked world, so I renounced them both as soon as I had become convinced that they were a delusion and were incapable of advancing what had to be achieved and what were the sole justification for their existence—human brotherhood and the ultimate humanizing of man. Neither has my country's past been entirely devoted to war and rebellion. Even the bloodshed and devastation that produced a turning point in my country's history, even this inevitable price for its advancement, gave an urgency and enduring quality to the longing for prudent, nonviolent, democratic solutions.

I must elucidate a little further, so that the reader will not confuse my ideas of reformism with what is commonly termed "social democracy," or confuse my nonviolence with that of Gandhi.

In the same way that I have always felt myself a Yugoslav and a Serb, or, rather, a Serb-Montenegrin, and have never been a Yugoslav integralist or nationalist, so from my earliest youth I have been an adherent of socialism and never a social democrat. I do not dispute that an impetus to my flow of thoughts, and an edge to my reasoning, may well have been given by the Yugoslav party leadership's contacts with social democrats, particularly with members of the British Labour party. This influence was strong at the time of the Yugoslav conflict with Moscow, and again, later, when efforts were made by the Socialist International to secure my release from prison. Yet my views have never been, nor are they today, identical with those of the social democrats. Although my present views and theirs seem, even to me, to differ only marginally on civil rights, and even less on personal freedom, the realities of Yugoslavia and the Communist world are such that the ways and means of achieving these freedoms can never be the same in Yugoslavia as they are in the West. No idea or program of action can be properly understood or given due consideration out of context. And although there can be no life struggle as we know it without ideas, the ideas themselves can never be much more than symbols, recognizable aspirations, whereas the real and practicable means for clearing the ground are formulas that people have to accept and enforce. Factions, parties, classes, society as a whole can, in theoretical terms, be freer under socialism than they are today in the West; but this can only be true if their grass roots are implanted in their own soil, in the particular Communist or post-Communist real situation and special ethos of each country separately. The reason is that in Communist countries it is not a matter of reforming a society where political freedoms already exist and where private ownership prevails, but the other way around—the society to be reformed lacks political freedoms and has a surfeit of public ownership. Obviously any exact identification of formulas for development and change in these two societies can take place only in the minds of dogmatists. Similarly, the role and importance of parliaments, parties, and governments cannot be identical, although on the surface and *pro forma* they may appear similar or even exactly the same in the two kinds of societies. As in every society undergoing change, only thoughtful and energetic forces can discover the suitable, vital formulas needed in a Communist society.

Similar conclusions can be drawn from comparisons of my nonviolent approach to Communism and Gandhi's *Satyagraha* (passive resistance) as a policy for changing society. I do not claim any exhaustive knowledge of Gandhi's outlook and tactics, but, as far as I understand them from reading his works and thinking about them in prison, I would say they are an expression of traditions peculiar to India and to the British colonial environment, as well as to his own particular religious outlook on society and human beings. What similarities are there between European, particularly Balkan, conditions and the situation in India? And the European (especially the Balkan) intellectual, reared in rebellion and violence, tempered by rationalist philosophy and dependent upon technical progress—in what ways could he identify himself with a philosophical forbearance in which time and the self have disappeared, and with disavowals of the priorities of industrialization to improve the human condition?

Two signs have dominated the firmament of twentieth-century man's aspirations and values—the stars of Lenin and Gandhi. These were the signs I followed in my youth and mature years. Gandhi's teaching, and, still more, his personality, became for me, particularly during my imprisonment, more than an example and an inspiration: they are a proof of the intuitive truth that our age has not fallen entirely under the curse of great demagogues and still greater despots, but is capable also of fostering great forbearance and co-operation and harboring not only mild evangelists but also dauntless martyrs. The examples of Hitler and Stalin may be taken as evidence that industrialized and industrializing societies provide the implements for coercion, while the personality and lifework of Gandhi show the imperishable and intransient nature of the longing for brotherhood and equity. A nonviolent, perfect society is not a possibility, but freer and more equitable societies are. The meaning and greatness of Gandhism are to be found in Gandhi's own personality. Gandhism, like every great idealist movement, disintegrated as soon as his successors had begun to savor the delights of power and riches. The events in my life and the flow of my thought so far described in this book are in themselves adequate to an understanding of why I was drawn to Gandhi early, even before my dispute with the party leadership, even before my revulsion from Stalinism and my doubts about the scientific infallibility and universal relevance of Marxist ideology. But there is another side to these experiences of mine—the reasons I was unable to become a disciple of Gandhi's on my own soil, where ways of life are marked by coercive dogmas. If an authentic interpretation of Gandhi's teaching were possible today, it seems to me that I would be right to embrace beliefs contrary to such dogmas, which is to say a belief in the awareness that no truths or objectives can justify the enslavement of a nation, or the torture of human beings, or the detruction of human life.

The maturation and clarification of my outlook took place gradually and on its own, under a distinctive impulse, in no way religious, but mainly, if not entirely, humanistic. I moved toward a new, undoctrinaire, un-idealized, existential humanism. When I use the word "humanism," I mean a continual analysis of, and reaction to, the human environment and to the demands and needs of human beings. It seems to me that we are witnessing the twilight of every kind of humanism that starts off with doctrinaire and theoretical hypotheses about the human being; this applies particularly to Communist humanism, which no one has ever explained properly, or ever will, although Communists overflow with love for the abstract "man of the future" while they are disenfranchising and neglecting the people about them. And when I use the word "existential," I am neither accepting nor rejecting contemporary existentialist philosophy, whether that of Jaspers or Sartre. I am pointing to rudimentary but complete human existence as being the touchstone and yardstick for all contemporary thinking that is genuinely humanist, and more particularly for all democratic and social activity.

Immediately after my release from prison in 1961, while working on the draft of *The New Class,* I jotted down the idea "conditional nonviolence," the thought at the back of my mind being the form of struggle and the means of transition from a Communist to a democratic system. These notes were confiscated at the time of my arrest at the beginning of April 1962. The detective's eye fell on those two words, and he asked me what they meant. I made a vague reply to the effect that they meant what they said. But while I was actually speaking I tended to distract my real meaning, which was this: in my view the use of violent, revolutionary ways and means against Communism was justified and unavoidable to the extent that the Communists themselves were using just such ways and means against democratic socialists and independent-minded men in their efforts to retain their dictatorial powers. But the detective went off on an errand at the order of his superiors, satisfied with my vague, perhaps confused, reply. Even so, my confusion, though only momentary, had revealed a weakness in me; and that I found galling. Until that moment (and the same is true since) I had always been frank about my own views; and this is largely the explanation for my stubbornness, on the one hand, and for the wrath of the party powers, on the other hand. This incident in the investigation, although it played no part in the later shaping of my outlook, was a crucial warning and a lesson that here was a matter on which my stand had to be clear and unambiguous.

I can now state, categorically and without reserve, that I am opposed to revolutionary means and the use of force in the struggle against Communism. The reformist and nonviolent approach to Communism is from the outset the main feature of my views and my method of struggle. And this is an attitude that applies to the struggle inside the various Communist countries as well as to relationships between Communist parties. Nevertheless, every Communist country has the right to defend itself, with arms if necessary, against onslaughts by other countries. Indeed, that is its bounden duty. This is because its very *raison d'être* lies in its right to provide its people with the means for living in their own way.

The roots of my attitude are to be found in my conception of Communism as being a revolutionary, *i.e.*, transitional, phase between a nonindustrial society and an industrial and postindustrial society. Although the Communists have always disposed of the national wealth as though it were their own, treating their fellow citizens as inferior creatures, they have never succeeded in establishing themselves as a class of either individual or collective landlords. The actual basic form of Communist ownership is power; and that cannot survive as a force in its own right, *i.e.*, outside the framework of social structures or even set against them. New patterns of ownership and new industrial relations are developing in Communist systems in spite of the Communists, breaking up ideological prejudices and bureaucratic stereotypes. Powerful, invincible, impregnable as a revolutionary movement and as an organization of violence, Communism has proved to be weak under so-called normal conditions and in free human situations. By banning other ideas and by demolishing all political structures other than its own, Communism has been undermining itself, because no human community can tolerate any kind of monotypical system except in exceptional circumstances, and even then it must be explicitly and unequivocally a vital historical necessity. Because it was first and foremost a power, a power of a particular kind—the power with history's mandate to carry out industrialization—Communism became enfeebled and superfluous once it had performed that task. The groups and ideas that have emerged from the society it built, and from its own ranks, may remain Communist in name for a longer or shorter period, but in essence they cease to be Communist in proportion to the degree of toleration they show toward other social groups and different points of view. Communism does not lose historic battles; it loses the battle of history, in spite of the fact, or perhaps precisely because of the fact, that it believed it held a knowledge of the laws of history.

But this does not mean that Communism will collapse of its own accord, and still less that the Communist potentates are waiting, impatiently, to hand over their power to someone else, even if that someone was a heretical, democratic blood brother hatched in the same brood. Everything that lives, everything that is human, falls not because it is rotten, but because it has been pushed by some newborn, new-tried force. There seems to be no reason why Communism should be the exception. New forces are emerging from the industrial society hacked into shape by Communism in an act of self-justification and justification in the eyes of history. At first they represent Communism's own uneasy conscience, but later they become a real force, variously closely knit or loosely organized, but certain of itself and self-conscious.

Most frequently, groups of intellectuals, like the Petöfi discussion club in Hungary in 1956 and the Writers Union in Czechoslovakia in 1968, are the first to wrest a certain amount of freedom of expression and action for themselves, and in so doing they set in motion the avalanche of a whole embittered society, a whole subjugated nation. It would appear from contemporary experiences that revolutionary organizations of the classic type—thoroughly conspiratorial, militarily disciplined, and ideologically united—are not essential. The sterility of dogmatism, the inertia of the ideological economy, and the monopoly of power, all lead inexorably to antagonism between Communists and people in all strata of society and give rise, in consequence, to the birth of new ideas and new movements in the heart of Communism itself as well as outside the system. It is as though it were all self-explanatory: what comes out of Communism is not in fact an entirely new, ideal society needing an all-embracing ideology for its "materialization"; it is only that the society in question escapes from the dogmatic strait jacket and from the monopolistic grip on the government and the economy held by a single ideological group. What is in a state of putrefaction is not the society as a whole, or the basic system of ownership rebuilt by the Communists after being plowed up by the Communist revolution, but, rather, Communist doctrine itself and the Communist structure of power. Removal of the Communists, the abolition of their monopoly over policy and the government, means in fact an end to the civil war they have been waging against society with their dogmas and privileges.

Revolution is not essential for victory over the Communist oligarchs and bureaucrats, because in fact victory over them is not the point at issue, nor is victory over the socialism behind which Communists are sheltered. Civil wars are even less necessary. However, recourse should be had to all other forms of struggle—demonstrations, strikes, protest marches, protest resolutions, and the like, and, most important of all, open and courageous criticism and moral firmness. All historical experience to date confirms this. What the West usually calls the Hungarian revolution (and the East calls the Hungarian counterrevolution) was in reality a national uprising against the intervention of the Soviet army, because Matyas Rákosi's reign of terror and the whole system of government had been previously overthrown without armed struggle. Similar conclusions can be drawn from the present situation in Czechoslovakia.

Such forms of struggle may be considered by some people to be revolutionary and their results a revolution. Perhaps these struggles are the revolutions of our time in the developed countries, or certain forms of these revolutions. Classic revolutions, revolutions that destroy social systems and systems of ownership, they are certainly not; no more so than the 1830 revolution in France, which should accurately be called a change of government. Societies in Communist systems today have no need of revolution, but they do need reformist movements and democratic changes of direction. The fact that Communist dogmatists and oligarchs will consider such changes of direction not merely counterrevolutionary but indeed the end of the world is of no consequence; those who behave as if they really were the masters of the world cannot help seeing things absolutely. I am reminded of a recent meeting with an old revolutionary who had spent ten years in Yugoslav prisons and camps, after the Soviet-Yugoslav dispute, for his support of Stalin and Soviet internationalism. In the course of our conversation I asked him how the situation looked to him today. "Very bad," he replied. "Sometimes it seems to me that there's some dialectical law by which matter itself is disintegrating and disappearing." To which I rejoined: "No, the world is where it has always been, and people are where they have always been. It is your ideas that are disintegrating and disappearing."

That, then, is the face of today's Communism in practice, and such are the prospects for change inside it and for society's emergence from it. Coercion as a force and the forms of coercion are more or less the same in all Communist countries, regardless of whether Communism came by way of internal, national revolution or by way of the instrumentality and intervention of the Soviet army. This is, of course, a generalized conclusion and, as such, not applicable to any particular Communist system or to a particular Communist country.

The greatest doubts about this kind of development appear when one looks at the Soviet Union, because of the lack of democratic traditions there, because of the hegemonic treatment of the non-Russian Soviet peoples by the Russian party bureaucracy, and because of the world role it has to play in relation to the other great powers. Nevertheless, I maintain that the people and nations of the Soviet Union, and in particular the Russian people and Russian nation, will achieve basic human and national rights without fratricidal bloodshed; and the most compelling reason is that this is the surest way for them to secure themselves against any *new* "ideal" ideologies or "liberating" despotisms, and the best guarantee that they will enjoy equality in the place that belongs to them in the comity of men and nations. Although pressures and resistances are more clear-cut and entrenched in the Soviet Union than elsewhere, even there new forces have been emerging in all areas of life, and new perceptions and imaginative outlooks are becoming apparent in the discontent of writers and intellectuals that is similar to that appearing in other East European countries. It is no accident that the thoughtful and sensitive Russian poet Andrei Voznesensky has remarked: "If we have something really new in Russia today, something that can really be called the product of a new society, it's this demand for poetry as a staple necessity. Poets have always been revered in Russia but never has there been anything like this." This demand is an expression of the people's increased need for a new sensibility and awareness, an expression made only by the writers, artists, and thinkers, because at present they alone are capable of doing so in such a confined and stifling atmosphere. They are always prophets of the new; in history it is no new thing that the great heretics are writers with a predilection for ideas, the poet-thinkers.

If the Russian people and the nations of the Soviet Union are lagging behind in liberalizing mass movements today, the same cannot be said of their intelligentsia. History stalks from nation to nation, and now that it has begun its walk through the Communist world, it would seem highly improbable that its "homeland," the Soviet Union, will be excluded from its itinerary. Every change in the Soviet Union will have its effect on European Communism, on Communism in the whole of the West, and it will cause radical changes in European relations and, more, in world relations. This is a job for

Russian and Soviet fighters for human freedom and democratic socialism. And I hope that I, too, will fight in this way for transformation in my country. Gomulka once repeated what someone else had said: "With wolves, one must howl." Let him do his howling. I shall not, though I have snarled and snapped with my teeth in my time. Such behavior achieves less than expected; and in any case there is no end to snapping and snarling. No ideal objective, no objective of any kind, is to be achieved by evil and oppressive means. An actual and practicable objective lies only in ways and means governed by human beings, the human condition. . . .

In one way or another freedom fighters in the Communist world (and freedom means the abolition of the party bureaucracy's monopoly) must have no less confidence in their ideas, their role, and their capabilities than the Communists had in their struggle for power. Though they may have diverse philosophies and points of view, and though they may come from different social milieus and from other walks of life, they have to be united in their direct, immediate aims—in their accessible, feasible means. This might be called the fanaticism of freedom, undogmatic dogmatism. So be it! For tomorrow the victors in their triumph will not be all that united; the new ends, the new means, the new ends-and-means will not be the same for all of them. Life is unique because it is not a monotype, and the hypothesis for every freedom is nonuniformity.

Without faith men cannot move wisps of straw, let alone mountains. One ideal dies that another may be born, manifestly "finer" and more "ultimate," and this is the human lot, for good or for ill. Those who are without faith, without self-dedication, are without hope and are entitled to nothing.

Though man may endure his ordeal like Sisyphus, the time must come for him to revolt like Prometheus, before his powers are exhausted by the ordeal.